Pottersville:
Where Is the Bailey Building and Loan?

by
Tom Pisapia

The contents of this work, including, but not limited to, the accuracy of events, people, and places depicted; opinions expressed; permission to use previously published materials included; and any advice given or actions advocated are solely the responsibility of the author, who assumes all liability for said work and indemnifies the publisher against any claims stemming from publication of the work.

All Rights Reserved
Copyright © 2017 by Tom Pisapia

No part of this book may be reproduced or transmitted, downloaded, distributed, reverse engineered, or stored in or introduced into any information storage and retrieval system, in any form or by any means, including photocopying and recording, whether electronic or mechanical, now known or hereinafter invented without permission in writing from the publisher.

Dorrance Publishing Co
585 Alpha Drive
Pittsburgh, PA 15238
Visit our website at *www.dorrancebookstore.com*

ISBN: 978-1-4809-4635-4
eISBN: 978-1-4809-4612-5

Preface

As I finished my strange three-year odyssey with the Resolution Trust Company/FDIC in the winter of '92/'93 and returned to my native Chicago, the realization hit that I had just closed and liquidated over a hundred savings and loans in the Southeast. The magnitude and irony of what I had just done had a dramatic impact on me, as I took inventory of my career, past, present, and future. I had just helped to erase the savings and loan industry. I knew that this process would continue until the industry was totally eliminated from the American culture. Someone had to tell the savings and loan story so that future generations would know of the enormous contribution that this industry had made to families, communities, and our country.

Introduction

Today, if someone were to *google* "savings and loan," the search would provide headlines that would scream the words "scandals," "fraud," "incompetence," and "political corruption," leaving the uninitiated with the impression that this industry deserved to be erased from the American landscape. I needed to write this book to clear the air and tell the real story of the sixty-five year savings and loan experiment.

The fact is that during its reign, the savings and loan industry directly employed hundreds of thousands of people in all fifty states and most U.S. territories, put millions of people into houses with long-term affordable fixed-rate mortgages, and those homes became subdivisions and suburbs, city blocks and towns. Those houses created billions in value and generational wealth and a real estate tax base that grew economies on the state, county, and city levels. Those taxes were needed to build roads, streets, schools, and hospitals. Police and fire departments had to be created to support all those homes that the S&Ls financed and the people that lived in them. The savings and loans were a cornerstone in the building of America.

Acknowledgements

I would like to thank Amelia Pisapia, Founder of *Mia Media*, for her support and guidance throughout the complex process of bringing this book to market. Thanks, Mia! Love you!

About the Author - Tom Pisapia

I have spent over forty years in the mortgage business. I took mortgages literally from Main Street (Sycamore, Illinois) to Wall Street (Merrill Lynch Capital Markets, Institutional side, Chicago/New York) and back again. Along the way I made stops at Fannie Mae, The Federal Home Loan Bank, the FDIC/RTC, numerous savings and loans, mortgage companies and, yes, even a few banks. Not surprisingly, for the final chapter (fifteen years) of my career, I migrated toward the credit union industry. The credit union "movement" gave me that same feeling of purpose and a greater good that I remembered from years before in the savings and loan industry.

I took 3,000 residential mortgage applications with pen and paper and closed over 2,000 of them at my desk with the same tools. I sold loans for cash, swapped for Fannie, Freddie, and Ginnie MBS, Dwarfs, Gnomes, and Midgets, did AOTs, CTOS and structured and sold pay through bonds, CMOs, and REMICs, anything that was anywhere close to a residential mortgage or even a convoluted derivative of one.

I think that I can bear witness to the savings and loan industry that served the economy well and fostered home ownership when no one else wanted the job, creating generational wealth for millions of Americans.

Dedication

To Gordie Carlson, the president of that little savings and loan who gave me a chance in a business that I knew nothing about, who taught me and gave me just enough rope to make my own mistakes and learn from them. He was my mentor and role model but, most importantly, my friend.

Table of Contents

Prologue xv

I "The Savings and Loan Crisis". 1
II The Journey Begins. 3
III The Growth of the Savings and Loan Industry 9
IV Deregulation Begins. 17
V The Demise of the Thrift Industry 31
VI The Birth of the RTC 47
VII The Journey Takes a Detour 63
VIII CenTrust Savings Bank, Miami, Florida 77
IX Even More Savings and Loan Debris 109
X The Aftermath and the Future 117

Prologue

Brief Synopsis of It's A Wonderful Life (1946) from Turner Classic Movies @TCM.com

On Christmas Eve, 1945, prayers are heard in heaven for George Bailey of Bedford Falls, New York. To help George, Clarence Oddbody, an angel who has not yet earned his wings, is being sent to earth to keep the despairing George from killing himself on this crucial night. To prepare him for his task, Clarence is shown George's life: As a child, George stops his younger brother Harry from drowning in an icy pond, then catches a bad cold and loses his hearing in one ear. Weeks later, George goes back to work at his after school job in Mr. Gower's drugstore and prevents Gower, who has gotten drunk after learning that his son has died of influenza, from accidentally dispensing arsenic-filled capsules to a sick child. George promises the remorseful Gower never to tell anyone about the incident and he never does. In 1928, as a grown young man, George, who has always dreamed of travel to exotic places, is about to leave on a world tour with money he has saved since high school. That night, at his younger brother Harry's high school graduation party, he becomes attracted to Mary Hatch, a girl who has secretly loved him since childhood. After a Charleston contest that results in an unscheduled splash into the school's swimming pool, they discuss their different ideas for the future until George's Uncle Billy comes for him with the news that his father has had a stroke. After Mr. Bailey's death, George's trip is canceled, but he still plans to leave for college until he learns that the board of directors of his father's financially tenuous building and loan society will not keep it open unless George manages it. Fearing that Mr. Potter, the town's richest and meanest man, will then have financial control of the town, George agrees to stay. Four years later, when Harry returns from college, financed by his brother, George again looks forward to leaving the stifling atmosphere of Bedford Falls and letting Harry run the business. However, when he learns that Harry has just married Ruth Dakin, whose father has offered Harry a good job, he again sacrifices his future to ensure Harry's. That night, George wanders over to Mary's house. Though he is adamant that he never intends to marry, he realizes that he loves her. Soon they are married, but as they leave for their honeymoon, a run on the bank convinces George to check on the building and loan. Because the bank has called in their loan, they have no money, only the honeymoon cash that Mary offers. Through George's persuasive words, most of the anxious customers settle for a minimum of cash, and they end the day with two dollars left. That night, Ernie the cab driver and Bert the cop show George his new "home," an abandoned mansion that Mary had wished for the night of the graduation dance. As the years pass, George continues to help the people of Bedford Falls avoid Potter's financial stranglehold as Mary rears their four children. On the day before Christmas, after the end of World War II, the 4-F George elatedly shows his friends news articles about Harry, who became a Medal-of-Honor-winning flier, while Uncle Billy makes an $8,000 deposit at the bank. Distracted by an exchange with Potter, Billy accidentally puts his deposit envelope inside Potter's newspaper, and Potter does not give it back when he finds it. Later, after Billy reveals the loss to George, they vainly search, while a bank examiner waits. Now on the verge of hysteria over the possibility of bankruptcy and a prison term for embezzlement, George goes home, angry and sullen. He yells at everyone except their youngest child Zuzu, who has caught a cold on the way home from school. He screams at Zuzu's teacher on the telephone, then leaves after a confrontation with Mary. He desperately goes to Potter to borrow the money against the building and loan, or even his life insurance, but Potter dismisses him, taunting him that he is worth more dead than alive. At a tavern run by his friend, Mr. Martini, George is socked by Mr. Welch, the teacher's husband. Now on the verge of suicide, George is about to jump off a bridge when Clarence comes to earth and intervenes by jumping in himself. George saves him, and as they dry out in the tollhouse, Clarence tells George that he is his guardian angel. George is unbelieving, but when he says he wishes that he had never been born, Clarence grants his wish. Revisiting Martini's and other places in town, George is not recognized by anyone and discovers that everything has changed. Harry drowned and Gower went to jail for poisoning the sick child. The town was renamed Pottersville and is full of vice and poverty. When George finally makes Clarence show him Mary, he discovers that she is a lonely, unmarried librarian. Finally, unable to face what might have been, George begs to live again and discovers that his wish is granted when Bert finds him back at the bridge. At home, an elated George is soon greeted by Mary, who has brought their friends and relatives, all of whom have contributed money to help him out. Harry arrives and offers a toast to his "big brother George, the richest man in town." As a bell on the Christmas tree rings, Zuzu says that every time a bell rings an angel receives his wings, and George knows that this time it was Clarence.

I guess that all of us, whether we want to admit it or not, get a little melancholy around Christmas time. And, in keeping with the spirit of the season, there probably isn't any better way to put the whole trauma in perspective than to watch a traditional holiday movie. You know the kind that I mean. Those that you've seen every year for at least the last twenty and you usually like to watch it alone because you still get a little choked up at the end. I think that It's A Wonderful Life really fits the bill for me and probably a lot of other people as well. All right, it's a little corny and I guess that it's pretty unbelievable in parts. Oh, I don't mean the part about the angel giving you an opportunity to see how the world would have been if you had never been born, I mean the part where all the people you've ever helped would really give a damn if you went to jail for embezzlement whether it was your drunken uncle's fault or not. I also know that the majority of us are much too cynical to think that a bank examiner would not press criminal charges even if you gave him a clothes basket full of money and sang him Christmas carols. And I personally know that you could never get a bank examiner to work on Christmas or, for that matter, most other times of the year that are much less significant. So I guess that you've got to put these realities aside for a few minutes and get caught up in the enthusiasm of the season and then it all seems quite plausible.

Well, I've watched the movie more than the required twenty times, and I still get a little misty at the end but not for the obvious reasons. I not only think that the movie is believable, but very prophetic. You see, in my version of the movie, George Bailey never wakes up from his dream. What he saw with the help of Clarence, his angel second class, was real. The Bailey Building and Loan doesn't exist anymore. It went out of business many years ago. Its paper was picked up by the greedy banker, Mr. Potter, for pennies on the dollar.

Pottersville: Where Is the Bailey Building and Loan?

George's little brother fell through the ice and drowned, every soldier on the ship died during the war, the drunken pharmacist poisoned the kid, and Donna Reed grew old as a spinster. You see, George Bailey never lived.

The portrayal of the Bailey Building and Loan may have been a little exaggerated but not by much. You see, in the beginning, it was a very simple concept, this whole Building and Loan idea. Groups of people got together with a common interest: they'd all like to own a home. Well, I don't think that we can find fault with their motives but buying a home was well beyond their means. These were just working people who lived week-to-week and would never be able to save enough money to buy a house. At the time, the only source of finance was commercial or mercantile banks. Banks at that time were much more interested with financing trade and commerce than making loans to individuals with questionable means. The idea of lending a sizeable some of money to a poor working stiff that had no assets and wanted to purchase something, a house, that didn't produce any income or predictable return on investment, was out of the question. As a result, the working class was forced to live in apartments usually owned by the same wealthy people that could get financing from banks. They were the ones who owned businesses and that fact qualified them to do business with the bankers of that era. The fact was that the rich did get richer and there wasn't any way for the working class to change this cycle. In addition, it wasn't unheard of for rents to be exorbitant and living conditions substandard. However, there wasn't any discrimination: both U.S. born and newly arrived immigrants were treated the same. They were all trapped in this poverty cycle that couldn't be broken. I guess that's what happens when the poor have no alternatives and no way to improve their station in life.

But let's start years before this movie was even made. Back to the late eighteenth century in England when building societies were first founded. A group of people got together and pooled their money so that they could build a house for one of their members. They repeated the process until every member had built a house. Once they each had one, there really wasn't any need for the building society anymore and they would simply close. Later on, these societies started to accept savings deposits from people whether they were looking to build a home or not and then these societies became permanent. The structure of these societies had one thing in common. They were all mutual organizations; that is, they were owned jointly by its borrowers and savers. Simply, they took the savers' money and used it to make home loans to its members.

This concept sounds so pure and innocent. George Bailey couldn't have done it better. No one at that time had ever heard of the danger of "borrowing short and lending long," or maturity mismatches, or the concept of asset and liability management.

Chapter I
"The Savings and Loan Crisis"

The internet is a wonderful source for all things relevant and irrelevant. It is amazing the wealth of opinions on, as they all seem to like to call it, "The Savings and Loan Crisis." Each critique on the "Crisis" builds a case for a different cause of the $160 billion + taxpayer expense.

- The underfunded FSLIC
- Jimmy Carter
- Paul Volker
- Michael Milken
- Corrupt S&L owners
- Wall Street
- Inept supervision
- Bad investments
- Real estate tax changes
- Brokered CDs (certificates of deposit)
- CPAs; and
- Lyndon Johnson and the Viet Nam War

No doubt there could be a little bit of truth in all of these causes and probably even a few more that I haven't mentioned but so much for this Monday morning analysis.

I do not plan on writing a textbook here. Let the academics write those pages with their theories and research galore, making sure that each event is documented and exact to the day, to the minute. Let those people who have never worked in the real world of finance during a "crisis," losing job after job as another S&L closed its doors, let them write those lofty thoughts in the safety of their academic castles.

I can only give you the reasons as they played out from my ringside seat, as I saw an industry that had mentored me slowly dissolve before my eyes. Then as a last stroke of irony, I was forced to preside over its burial at the RTC. This is my story, take it or leave it.

I've included a brief timeline of some of the bigger events during this period in the back of the book (Appendex I, Page 125). Those few dates and facts are noted but, in truth, they really don't matter. The only meaningful fact is that this *did* happen and it didn't need to happen.

Chapter II
The Journey Begins

It was a cold January sixty miles west of Chicago when I was out of school and out of work. I had just finished a three-year job at a college bar after I dropped out of grad school and was looking for something a little more stable. I received a call from the president of the local savings and loan who had a piece of the mortgage on my last employer's bar building and he asked me to come in for an interview. It was a small savings and loan with barely one additional branch office and about $30 million in assets. The president was looking for a loan officer and collection manager and, after the interview, he asked me to drop off a list of the college business courses I had taken. I wasn't really interested in the job and, thinking back, I didn't know that there even was a difference between banks and savings and loans at that time. I guess that there was plenty of time over the next few decades to learn that lesson. I dropped off the list of business courses that I had taken at the drive up window a few days later (showing how aggressively I was pursuing this position) and, as luck would have it, I got the job.

It was early March 1976, and for the next five months I sat at a desk in front of the president's office and read books about the function of savings and loans, regulations, deposits, mortgage loans, and home ownership. I took some courses and, within eighteen months, became the manager of the loan department. Over the next six years I took over 3,000 mortgage applications with pen and paper, I closed over 2,000 mortgage loans at my desk, all hand-typed with carbon paper copies, and even collected a number of delinquent mortgages without ever resorting to foreclosure. I learned construction lending, acquisition and development of residential homes and condominiums, appraisal and lending theory, and even created and taught the mortgage finance course at the local college. I was president of the local Jaycee chapter, vice-president of the Chamber of Commerce and taught a mortgage lending class for people from other savings and loans. I was comfortable that I had found a career in an industry that had a history and a future and I knew that I wanted to be a part of it. That president saw something in me and gave me a chance in a business that I knew nothing about. He was my mentor then and still is today. His little shop has been taken over by two different banks and even a thrift (another name for a savings and loan) but he stayed there at the same location doing basically the same things throughout all of these changes until he reached retirement. Maybe I should have stayed there too. In retrospect, it wouldn't have been so bad.

In those early years in the business, I learned a great deal about regulation. The thrift industry in that era had a regulation for everything. Between the Federal Home Loan Bank Board and the Federal Savings and Loan Insurance Corp. (FSLIC), we were told what products we could offer, what we could pay for deposits, and even what we could charge on mortgages.

The savings product was simple; it was a passbook savings account. The mortgage was simple. It was a twenty-nine-year fixed-rate loan.

You probably are wondering why it was a twenty-nine-year loan. Well, you see, we had a book that had various rates and amortization terms by month, and it would tell you what the principle and interest payment was per $1,000 of loan balance. But it was easy to sometimes to write down the wrong figure as you ran your finger along the page. Since the only machine we had was an adding machine, there wasn't any chance of doing present value calculations.

My sense was that, since loans could not amortize for more than thirty years by regulation, we picked twenty-nine to make sure that even if we made a small mistake, it would still be paid off in thirty years or less. It was a rather quaint approach to compliance, but it was totally consistent with that era.

The rate was simple; we had a usury law in Illinois that capped what we could charge and that rate was given to us monthly by the state. This was a pretty simple game; everyone, that is savings and loans, were all on the same level playing field. The only things that separated one thrift from the next was the quality of service and, of course, what type of gift you gave depositors for opening a new account. These "premiums" really became big business. Since this was the only differentiating element among thrifts, some even put out catalogs to describe the various household appliances or trinkets you could receive based on the size of your deposit. The premium competition in Chicago became so intense during this period, that one good-size thrift converted its lobby into a showroom for its wares. The result looked like a department store with teller windows. It even had a cash register at the front door just in case the premiums weren't totally free and you needed to make a little cash contribution. Even the cost of these "inducements" was regulated. The fed wanted to make sure that you weren't buying deposits. That seems almost quaint by current standards, but that was a genuine concern of regulators in a totally regulated environment. This was a very innocent time in the history of thrifts. Can you imagine committees that spent the majority of their

5

time discussing the pros and cons of toasters and electric blankets rather than asset and liability management? I can, and I'm not referring to any particular thrift, rather an entire industry. It was a simpler time. The overwhelming majority of your assets had to be used to finance the purchase, construction, or refinance of residential dwellings. It was kind of noble. I mean you put people in houses. They made their payments to you every month, usually in person. They had kids and sent them to school. They paid their taxes. Then their kids grew up and they wanted to buy a house too. Sure, you were getting paid to do this, but people benefitted from what you were doing. Realtors sold, builders built, plumbers plumbed; it was good for the economy.

These home mortgages that the thrifts were making never moved during that era. They were as immobile as the houses that secured them. When a loan was made, it was put on the books and there it stayed. The borrowers made their payments to you each month and at the end of twenty-nine years or so, you handed them a canceled note marked "PAID IN FULL." That document showed the world that they owned their house free and clear. It was everyone's goal to get that piece of paper. It was the culmination of a lifetimes work. Oh yes, we did prepare a mortgage release document, hand-typed of course, and then we would drive to the local county courthouse and hand-deliver that document to be recorded and release the lien on that property.

At that time, it was unheard of to sell someone's mortgage. The borrower fully expected to make his payments at the same location and to the same people until the debt was satisfied. After all, you gave him the money and he would pay you back. If the loan were sold, it would be taken quite personally by the borrower. It was like saying that he wasn't a good customer and usually would result in the closing of all of his accounts plus some less than favorable public commentary. Working in the borrower's favor was the lack of a standardized conduit to sell these mortgages anyway. There was, of course, the Federal National Mortgage Association (Fannie Mae) and the new Federal Home Loan Mortgage Corp. (Freddie Mac) but these were primarily used by mortgage bankers, large banks and only the very largest of the savings and loans. Consequently, if your loan was to be sold, it would be done on a private placement basis with another savings and loan that had extra cash that needed to be invested in home loans as well. It wasn't an uncommon practice to sell only the best loans to another shop and to "unofficially" repurchase or substitute a "good" loan for any one that did not pay regularly. It was a gentleman's game. You certainly wouldn't want the word to get around that you had sold someone a bad loan. Thrifts went one step farther and would pool a group of loans together and sell a percentage of that pool to another shop (savings and loan). They would then retain a percentage of that pool for themselves, further showing that these loans are so good that I'm keeping some for myself. And, most importantly, your borrowers could continue to make their payments to you. Then you would pass on a pro-rata piece of that remittance to the other S&L. These rather awkward arrangements were appropriately called "participations," and they will be revisited later in this tale.

Due to this limited and unpopular practice of selling loans, there were times that loan demand would exceed the available funds to make them. It wasn't uncommon to become "loaned up." You would then take your shop out of the mortgage market by raising your rates just enough to make them unattractive until your loan repayments and new deposits caught up. But everyone, even realtors, understood that. That was a small price to pay for keeping everything local. When you became flush again, you would get back in to the mortgage business until the next time.

The "status quo" was the order of the day. These were "mutual" savings and loans. Everyone that had a savings account automatically received votable shares in the thrift. The more money you had on deposit, the more mutual shares you received. If you had sizeable deposits, you could even get voted on to the Board of Directors. Most Boards were made up of a cross-section of the community that they served. You usually had a businessman or two, a teacher, a professional type either doctor or lawyer, a farmer if you were rural, and a realtor or someone else that had sizeable real estate holdings. These appointments were certainly not for the money, which was usually just a stipend, but for the prestige that they represented in the community. Most depositors simply signed the proxy cards that were sent to them in advance of the annual meetings and never gave it a second thought. No dissident shareholders, no proxy fights, no raucous shareholders meetings, just a group of "good old boys" listening to the same stale reports and moving the same stale motions. Not usually much moving and shaking, just the same accolades being passed around year after year. You see, there weren't any dividends paid to shareholders either. So if the ship was still upright and your last examination went well, we'll see you at the next meeting. This regulation was great! It was the old "3, 6, 9" rule. Pay "3 percent" for your deposits, lend it out at "6 percent," and be on the golf course by "9." Life was good. No one could have foreseen what was about to happen and, even if they could, they were ill prepared to cope with the changes that were about to come.

Chapter III
The Growth of the U.S. Savings and Loan Industry

After the end of World War II, the demand for housing exploded. As millions of our returning servicemen re-entered the work force, they looked to start families and buy houses and so the "baby boom" began. Then the construction of the Interstate Highway system under Eisenhower in the '50s not only created much-needed jobs but allowed for expansion outside of the cities and "suburbia" was born.

The savings and loan industry was in the perfect place to take advantage of this housing windfall, and they did. Not only did they become the centerpiece of the housing boom but competed with banks for deposits as well. And by 1980 there were over 4,000 savings and loans in the U.S. with assets of $600 billion, and $480 billion of those assets were in mortgage loans.

Having always been on the savings and loan side of the ledger, I guess that I really never paid much attention to commercial banks unless I needed to borrow from them. I assumed that they had their role to play in this finance game and the savings and loans had theirs. You would get a business loan or checking account from a Bank, a house loan from a savings and loan, and, if you had a local credit union, get a car loan from them.

I knew what their different charters enabled each of them to do as well as what they were each prohibited from doing. I knew that something called the Regulation "Q" differential allowed thrifts to pay an extra twenty-five basis points on deposits. That always seemed to be a fair trade off for the long-term fixed-rate mortgages that the thrifts made. After all, commercial banks didn't want anything to do with those long-term fixed-rate maturities. They liked things that floated with their "prime" rate and "ballooned" every few years. They liked making short-term commercial loans with hefty equity positions. Heck, they liked checking accounts and all that "free" money, and they were the only game in town for that instrument. Everybody had to have a checking account; even if you had a mortgage at a savings and loan, you still had to write a bank check to make your monthly payment. Well, I guess that the banks didn't like how pushy the savings and loans had gotten. They weren't the Bailey Building and Loans anymore. They had gotten bigger and a little more aggressive and, worst of all, they became a competitor. Wait a minute, that doesn't make any sense. The savings and loans didn't even have any shareholders to answer to, no quarterly dividends to pay, and no fear of losing their jobs after back-to-back bad quarters. There must have been some other reason.

The banks did indeed get some real competition from the large West Coast thrifts and the East Coast savings banks, but what about the thousands of little thrifts across the country that were still in the Building and Loan motif? Well, that was too bad; they all had to be painted with the same brush.

What had these thrifts done that had so infuriated these huge commercial banking icons, the descendants of the mercantile banking empires? Well, first they started to mimic the bankers' approach to cheap deposits and began offering their own version of checking accounts. But they were forbidden from using any of the banking terms that the public was accustomed to. They called their clone "Negotiable Orders of Withdrawal" or NOW accounts. Well, if it looks like a duck and acts like one, and it did. Eventually you could use these NOW accounts just like any checking account that you had ever seen. Even merchants starting accepting them as a "Negotiable" instrument. The thrifts had overstepped their bounds, and the commercial bankers were not going to let them get away with it.

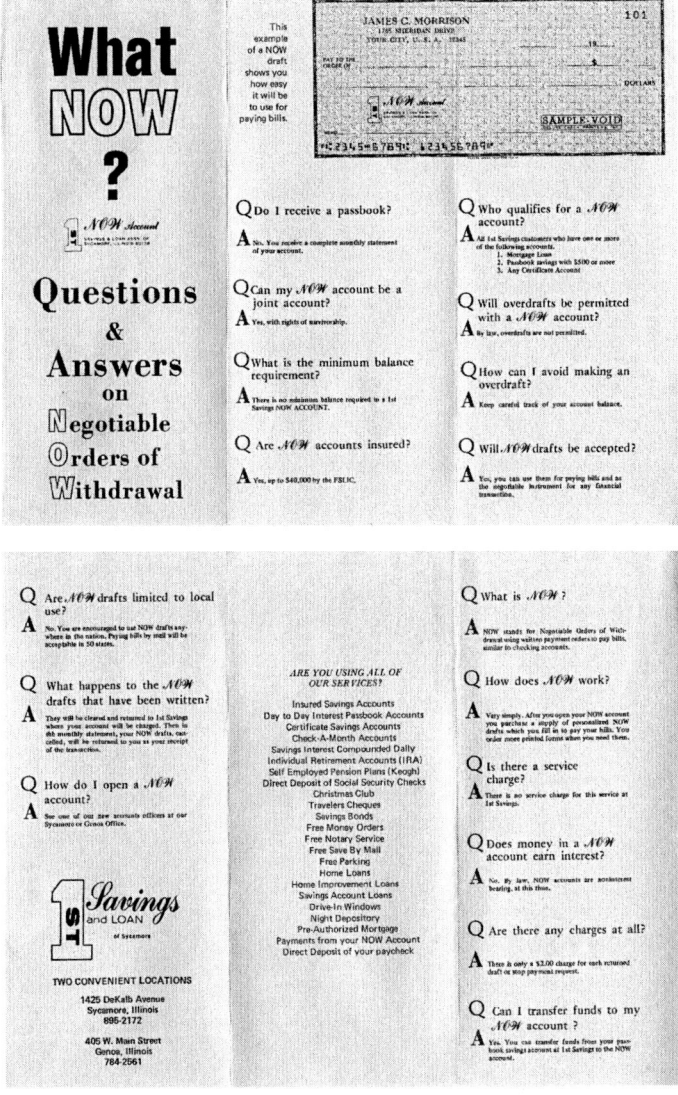

A fun note is that these NOW accounts were insured to $40,000 by the FSLIC, which of course was the maximum deposit insurance at the time ☺

But, what could the banks do to get even with the thrifts and, at the same time, not look like the bad guys? It was simple. Let the thrifts do it to themselves. Now that the thrifts were fairly confident that they could run financial institutions, they were an easy mark. They had begun to think that they were over-regulated and could do a better job of governing their own shops if they had more latitude. The time was right.

Very early on in my thrift education process, I learned a word that struck fear in every savings and loan executive's heart. It was the modern day equivalent of the run on the Bailey Building and Loan. However, in this case, they didn't have a lobby full of irate customers trying to withdraw their hard-earned savings. This was a much more subtle approach and simply involved depositors withdrawing some or all of their money and buying U.S. Treasury bills, notes, or bonds. This was termed "disintermediation." I've never had such fun with a word that had never even been used in a "G" rated movie's theme song. But this was a real fear for all financial institutions of that era. That fear was that retail customers would bypass the financial intermediaries (banks and thrifts) and invest directly in government securities. While having their rates set by the regulators, they feared that higher paying Treasuries would lure their deposits away. If they could only set their own rates, they were sure that they could prevent this loss of "cheap" money. The stage was set, and this was the opportunity that the bankers were looking for to begin their revenge.

(I guess there is a certain bit of irony in that all financial institutions also sell U.S. Savings Bonds, but they were never really viewed as a threat of any magnitude. This was just something to buy the grand kids when you didn't know their sizes anymore.)

Of course, throughout this period I didn't know that any of this turmoil was going on. I was still working for that little thrift doing the things that little thrifts of that era were doing. I worked my "9 to 5," five days a week and every other Saturday from 9 to 1. I was taking mortgage applications daily, processing those loans, and presenting them to a loan committee for approval. The approval process at that time reflected the "hands on" attitude that permeated the industry. Each loan would be presented to a three person loan committee that was made up of the President and senior management.

This group met twice per week and would individually review each loan and use a very subjective approach in deciding whether to approve or reject the applicant. Since this was a small town, the committee knew most of the borrowers or at least one or more of their relatives. They may have dealt with them in the past, gone to their church, or grown up with them. It was the personal touch, and I would rather rely on their instincts and input than any numeric ratios. It wasn't unusual to get comments like "his father never paid a bill on time" (reject the loan) or "they're good people, I knew his grandfather" (make the loan). That was a time when we knew how to work together. If I got a call from the President in advance of the meeting, I knew that he wanted a particular borrower approved. In that case, I was the one to convince the other members to approve the loan. It had to look like it was my idea. Maybe none of us at that time had read any Machiavelli, but we knew how to make a system work. Sure, there were borrowers that no one knew and, in that event, we actually looked at their credit and ability to repay the loan and made a decision based on the facts. But anyone could do that. Objectivity can be done by anyone. Objectivity is something that can be done by any number of automated underwriting programs currently being touted by Fannie Mae, Freddie Mac, or numerous private entities. That's not what this was about. This was about putting people in homes that should be in homes. This was about the town, the community, the neighborhood.

At that time there was even an attempt to standardize this whole approval process, to reduce the numerous intangibles of underwriting to

13

a mere credit score. I discuss this now because this approach reflected the attitudes and predispositions of the time. Not with any malice but merely as a mirror of the then current thought. A credit scoring sheet was created, similar to those used by most lenders. Various borrower characteristics were listed and each was given a point value. Age, occupation, marital status, number of children, credit, and gross income.

- *Age* - thirty to fifty years old was the highest point value. If you were younger or older, points were subtracted;
- *Occupation* - professionals scored best, followed by skilled tradesmen, unskilled, clerical, retired, and the unemployed;
- *Marital Status* - married was best, then unmarried, divorced, widowed, and separated. Each with declining point values;
- *Number of Children* - one or two was good but you lost points for additional kids;
- *Credit* - good credit scored well but bad credit or no credit lost you points; and
- *Gross Income* - under $15,000 wasn't good but as the income went up so did the points.

After the scoring was complete, the points were totaled up. The higher the score, the better chance of approval. Obviously all of this was done prior to the Equal Credit Opportunity Act (ECOA) and, in light of the current standards for lending, we had violated about every condition for the extension of credit ever thought of, with the exception of race. This attempt at standardization did not use race as any component. If the scores looked good, the loan was made. But what about that subjectivity I mentioned earlier? Well, sometimes subjectivity is a good thing. As in the case of a seventy-two-year-old black minister of a local congregation that neither had the verifiable income, credit, or age qualification. The committee didn't hesitate to approve that loan. After all, he was good for the community so disregard the above. A few weeks later, as I closed his loan at my desk, I explained the mortgage codicil regarding the payments that he would be required to make. As I covered that paragraph, he blessed me for giving him that thirty-year fixed-rate loan and hoped that, if it was God's will, he would be happy to make that last payment to me as he celebrated his 102nd birthday. I guess that it really wasn't that bad a system after all. During the six years that I presented loans to that committee, I never saw one instance of discrimination. If it was a good loan, let's make it, and we did.

Meanwhile, the bankers down the street and across the nation were doing about the same things that we were doing, but their anger at the thrifts continued to grow.

Chapter IV
Deregulation Begins

Banks were mad as hell about Regulation "Q," they were mad about NOW accounts, they were mad about the thrifts' intrusion into their space. They wanted the thrifts to be on a level playing field with no advantages at all. They even had support from some large thrifts and savings banks that were ready to take off the gloves. It was time to let the thrifts fend for themselves. The timing was great. During that period everything was being deregulated. The airlines, trucking, and phone industries had been or were about to be put into the new competitive arena of deregulation. The financial industry now sounded like a natural to join them.

The irony was that the thrift industry went along with the proposed deregulation sequence. In some ways I really think many of the thrifts thought they could handle it or maybe their voices just weren't loud enough to be heard over those of the big thrifts.

Well, basically the bankers got their wish as a result of just two regulatory events. The first event was in ***April 1981*** when the Federal Home Loan Bank Board (FHLBB) lifted the prohibition on making adjustable-rate mortgages (ARMs) for Federal Thrifts. Now, for the most part, you might say "this doesn't sound like a bad thing." And had the regulators stopped right there and waited maybe ten or fifteen years, I would agree. I believe that had they stopped there for an extended period of time, there might not have ever been a savings and loan crisis. You see, as noted earlier, S&Ls were making thirty-year (or twenty-nine year) fixed-rate loans on residential properties. These loans didn't pay off very fast and especially in a rising rate environment. And, at this time during the Carter administration, rates were hitting the highest levels that I have ever seen before or since.

If the thrifts had been given a reasonable period of time to replace those long-term fixed-rate loans with adjustable-rate mortgages, they may have had at least a fighting chance of surviving, but that was not to be.

Soon after the FHLBB pronouncement, the thrift industry and the GSEs (Government Sponsored Enterprises) – namely, Fannie Mae and Freddie Mac – began working on just what went into a good ARM; you know, all those pesky little details like indexes, adjustment caps, life time caps, margins, start rates, temporary buy downs, amortization, negative amortization, initial term 1,3,5,7,10, and pricing. Well, everybody had an opinion on what should go in to the mix. The West Coast liked the 11th District of the Federal Home Loan Bank cost-of-funds index (COFI), the Midwest liked the 7th District, some liked various T-Bills, prime, LIBOR and about anything that moved. No one could agree on mortgage documents either, and the GSEs had not stepped up yet to standardize anything.

The final irony for an industry trying to find the perfect ARM was that borrowers didn't like ARMs. They had grown accustomed to the fixed-rate mortgage that they had and their parents had before them. It would take many years for the thrift industry to learn how to make ARMs and even longer for the public to accept them. Once again, time was not on the side of the thrifts.

(As an aside, many years later during an RTC closure of a Florida S&L, we discovered an ARM portfolio that was tied to PHILS. I was curious enough to ask an employee where I could get the current index, but I was told that PHIL no longer worked there).

While all this was going on, the other deregulation shoe dropped on **October 15, 1982**, Garn-St. Germain (just about a year and a half after the first one).

Remember that the biggest fear of the day was disintermediation, that customers would bypass the financial intermediaries and invest directly in Treasuries. Well, Garn-St. Germain was going to fix that problem and many others.

Financial institutions were now going to be able to pay market rates on a six month certificate of deposit. This instrument became known as the Money Market Certificate (MMC). This seemed to be a relatively harmless way to retain low cost deposits. Simply set these rates weekly based on the movement of comparable Treasuries and you won't get "disintermediated" that is, lose your deposits. No one had any idea of what to do with the money they raised or retained. But at least it wasn't going away. Besides, thrifts always made long-term fixed-rate mortgages with short term deposits. That was the way it had always been done. Why should anything change just because this "deregulation" thing was being implemented? Nobody seemed to notice or care at that time that they were being deregulated backwards. That is, the liability side (deposits) of the ledger was allowed to float while the entire industry sat on long-term fixed-rate portfolios of mortgage loans on the asset side. The industry had a total of eighteen months between the lifting of the ARM prohibition and the beginning of the money market rate cost of funds.

Then, as if it were choreographed by the banking industry, rates started to rise. As they went to 7 percent, thrifts dutifully raised their rates to retain deposits. Then they went to 8, 9, 10, 11, you get the picture. Each time they went up, the rates on the Money Market Certificates went up. All of a sudden, thrifts were paying more for these short-term deposits than they were getting on their investment portfolios. They were upside down. What did they think they could do, compete with the Federal government to attract deposits and in an inflationary market cycle? If the Fed needs money to retire old borrowings and raise fresh cash, and they do every week, don't you think that it will pay whatever is necessary to get those funds? Could there be a greater evil than disintermediation? There sure was. But now it was too late. The thrifts were sitting on "hot," six-month, high-rate deposits with nowhere to invest to show a positive spread over their costs. Since their portfolios were primarily fixed and long-term, they couldn't look to those borrowers for relief. So, in their rush for positive earnings, they started to look for investments that yielded more than their costs. Commercial loans, acquisition and development loans, automobile paper, plus any number of products that Wall Street was happy to offer seemed to fit the bill. It didn't seem to matter that they were making loans that they didn't have the expertise to make. How hard could it be? They were lenders. They made home loans. It must be the same. The same attitude prevailed when they bought loans that they didn't know how to evaluate. They bought time share paper out of the vacation belts. Whether it was Colorado or Broward and Dade Counties in Florida, it all worked. They couldn't get enough of condo paper from the oil rich states, especially condos along the Houston corridor. They bought paper on hotels, motels, strip shopping centers. Anything that looked like real estate and had a good yield. At that time diversity meant different states for different vacations under the guise of making inspections on your investments. I guess that not even banks like the now deceased Continental Bank of Chicago and Penn Square in Oklahoma were immune.

 I know these things firsthand. By this time I had left the little savings and loan behind and gone to work for a private mortgage insurance company as a whole loan trader. (By the way, private mortgage insurance [PMI] is the coverage that lenders require when a borrower has less than a 20 percent down payment on a conventional loan.) This company along with most other private mortgage insurance companies just wanted to sell insurance. They didn't know nor really care what the secondary market was, but they knew that if they did these loan placements for their customers (banks, mortgage bankers, and thrifts), they stood a very good chance of getting their mortgage insurance business. My job was to put buyers and sellers of mortgage loans together. As a trader in the Midwest, most of my customers were thrifts that had cash. The Midwest in the early '80s was experiencing more of a recession than a boom, and all the growth was in the Southeast, Southwest, and West. My counterparts in my trading group were based in not only all the strategic growth areas but coast-to-coast. If my customers wanted specific product or locations, I could get it. At that time, the oil and vacation belts couldn't get enough capital to fuel their growth and my customers couldn't wait to get their capital to work. I would take an order from one of my customers and put it out across our system. My fellow traders would then call me with their offerings. I would then present these deals to my customers and act as the middleman in shuttling questions and answers before they made direct contact with each other. It was an easy game then with motivated buyers and sellers, and we were happy to put them together without even charging them a dime for the service. Just send us some of that private mortgage insurance business.

 I found these hungry buyers all the paper that they wanted, and I got paid for doing it. Mine wasn't to pass judgment on loan quality, only to make marriages, and I did.

 But we weren't the only ones providing this service. Lenders with capital were bombarded with solicitations from private brokerage companies, direct from sellers of product, and let's not forget Wall Street. Each had his own agenda, and it was always the same whether it was money or mortgage insurance. No one ever looked out for the buyers; the "caveat" was squarely in the "emptor's" court. After all, they were running financial institutions; they were supposed to know what they were doing.

These buyers of product had more than just yield in mind when they sought out potential loan acquisitions. Sure, they had money that they needed to invest and show their respective Boards that they were doing a good job, but what was the harm in spreading their investments around. Let's buy some ski resort loans, some Florida vacation paper, and, oh yes, some California loans near my daughter's house. Not only were their Boards convinced that the CEOs were exercising good judgment by spreading their investments around, but by visiting each investment quarterly, they could keep an eye on what they had bought. This was a fun time for CEOs. They got paid vacations on top of paid vacations, and their naive Boards lacked the business acumen to offer any guidance.

This buying and selling game wasn't just for the medium and large players either. There were many small thrifts that wanted in on the action as well. They had the same problems that all of their thrift brethren shared, but they had even less expertise in this and most other areas. But there was even an answer for their dilemma. Since they knew many other medium-sized shops that were buying product, they would simply buy a piece of the loan pools that had already been purchased. Why not, they were bigger shops that must certainly know what they were doing. These little shops didn't even get to attend the conventions and share in the quarterly visits. But they too had investments on their books that showed a positive spread for now. And so the poison spread from the large to the medium to the small thrifts.

I think that what most clearly dramatized the capital frenzy during this period was the secondary market conferences. These events were sponsored either by the Mortgage Bankers or Savings and Loan trade associations. Both of these groups held one each nationally but local or state groups also held their own functions. What they all had in common was a "supermarket place." An area that during each conference was reserved for all participating lenders and vendors to show their wares. Whether sellers of loans, private mortgage insurance, lending services, or banking hardware, they would actually set up booths to call attention to their products. Some lenders used tastefully made brochures and gave out customized trinkets to get noticed. At one event in Hawaii, a high flying California mortgage banking company had a little Wheel of Fortune to determine what trinket you would win when you visited their booth, but what made their display different is that they had the real Vanna White spinning it for you! (I never knew she was so tiny.)

(That would be my ex-wife, Cheryl, with Vanna and, of course, yours truly! C'mon, it was Hawaii and the shirt was appropriate! Notice the little wheel of fortune in the background)

Others, however, were much less subtle and brought actual loan files with them. Not just a few, but boxes of loans that were currently being made through their construction subsidiaries. I personally helped one now-defunct Texas lender carry his boxes out to his car as the conference adjourned. They had fully expected buyers to analyze those loans and be prepared to make decisions by the time they returned to their respective shops. After all, it was first come, first served, and there were a lot of dollars chasing a dwindling number of "good" investments. The private secondary market had hit an all-time low. Loans were being hawked like so many rings and watches on a street corner.

For a short period, things went fine. The loans were performing and the thrifts were booking record profits. But, as always occurs when more dollars are chasing fewer investments, the quality started to diminish. Soon payments on loans became slow. Projects began folding up. Construction was stopping, even on incomplete projects.

Dallas/Ft. Worth, Houston, Broward, Dade Counties in Florida, and the entire State of California all became words that the remaining investors preceded by the word "No" when looking for loans. On some thrift ledgers everything still looked pretty good. The investments were yielding more than the cost of funds, but then the payments stopped. The thrifts had done what they had set out to do. They had stopped disintermediation. Why should depositors withdraw their funds when they were getting money market rates at their corner savings and loan?

Yes, they kept their deposits and learned a new term, default risk. Now instead of having a positive return on their investments, they had no return at all and, worst yet, they had lost their original capital.

Not all thrifts looking for this positive arbitrage (spread) were as reckless as the whole loan buyers of the era. Some did look for security and guaranteed returns on their investments. Many tried investing in mortgage backed securities which were guaranteed by Fannie Mae, Freddie Mac, or Ginnie Mae (Government National Mortgage Association). However, the trade off was a lower yield than they could get on whole loan investments. Still some thrifts found that the safety was worth the reduction in yield. Here again the little shops found that they didn't even have the expertise to do that right. Since these shops were so small, they didn't have access to the reputable (?) primary dealers in New York. You wouldn't catch a Salomon Brothers or Goldman Sachs picking up your call unless you had $300 million in assets and that would probably be by some junior trader. Instead their coverage from the investment banking community was left to the regional dealers. These were dealers that cleared their transactions through one of the *primary dealers** of the time. This was a second tier of investment bankers that picked up the scraps that the big houses wouldn't bother with. These regional firms came from Tennessee, Arkansas, Florida, Texas, the Midwest, and California. They had sprung up in almost every state, especially where the securities laws were most lax. Some were no more than "boiler room" operations with phone banks and hungry commissioned salesmen with trade directories in hand. Many of these salesmen, or "bond bandits," as they were later called, didn't know much about the products that they were selling but they knew that there were big spreads, and commissions, when you dealt in an inefficient market or with less-than-savvy customers. In this case they had both. They had no trouble padding these investments with a little extra for themselves, well above industry spreads. These little thrifts didn't have a Telerate (showing my age) on their desks nor did they have other investment bankers to give them competing offers. And, if the instrument wasn't commonly traded, the price was whatever the broker said it was. These thrifts were at the mercy of these middlemen who flattered them and made them feel like they were "players."

As the regionals gained the confidence of these small players, they became their sole source of information and direction. They developed a bond, and the thrifts became an easy mark for many of the less than reputable dealers. The thrifts became a dumping ground for numerous mortgage and non-mortgage instruments that were totally inappropriate investments. It was during this period that a new instrument was born that looked and smelled like a mortgage investment but it was the step child of mortgages, as we knew them. It was the mortgage derivative. A straight forward instrument in its early days, as in the case of agency mortgage backed securities (MBS), it became one of the least understood investments of our time. Sure, the underlying collateral might have been fully guaranteed mortgage backed securities, but what happened to the cash flows that formed the pieces or traunches that were sold off was a very different investment animal. Even the creators of the instruments, the Wall Street dealers, couldn't fully explain how these investments would work under most interest rate environments. They were touted as safe and liquid but the "creator" was usually the only one willing to buy them back and, if he did, only at his price. I learned this lesson first hand many years later as I analyzed and sold these same instruments to the Street while liquidating S&L portfolios for the Fed. They were just a few of the remnants left by numerous defunct savings and loans that I was to liquidate posthumously. It was no wonder that the ill-equipped Federal regulators would wrestle with the same questions later and still find no answers.

- *A **primary dealer** is a firm that buys government securities directly from a government, with the intention of reselling them to others, thus acting as a market maker of government securities.*

Sometimes even when these small shops decided to buy appropriate investment instruments, they still got into trouble. They were, of course, still dealing with the regional brokers who they trusted when they decided to buy mortgage backed securities. Since these securities offered less yield but were guaranteed, they would take advantage of any additional spread they could garner. And, when these fine brokers offered to pay them a small additional spread, usually not more than 1/8 of a point, if they didn't take delivery of the securities, the thrifts jumped at the chance. This was like found money for the thrifts. By merely saving the broker the time and cost of having the security issued in the thrift's name they were able to pick up some extra yield. Well, as you might imagine, these brokers were able to do the same thing with numerous thrifts who also wanted to get a little additional yield, and all the broker had to do was to send each of them a monthly statement plus the small principal and interest payment that was due and everyone was happy.

That is, everyone was happy until some thrift decided, either on its own or at the urging of its regulator, to take possession of that security that had already bought and paid for. That's when the schemes started to unravel. Sometimes that fine broker had actually sold that same security to a number of small thrifts who all showed the same identification number (CUSIP)* on their books. And, in some cases, there wasn't even any security purchased at all. So, down went the broker and down went all those little shops that had given their trust to these middlemen.

In one specific instance, during this period, I remember sitting across from a thrift executive that I had known for many years who had fallen victim to this exact scheme. His failure to take possession of a security was about to cost him his job of twenty years, his standing in the community, his family's reputation, and would surely result in the collapse of the savings and loan that had employed him. There was little solace that I could give him at that point. This was a man that had worked very hard for a very long time. He had started at the bottom and worked his way up. It was the American dream for him. He had achieved the respectability and prominence that was due him. He was a man that would never think of buying a pair of shoes without taking them with him but became a man that would buy a million dollar security from someone that he didn't know and had never met and agree to let them hold it for him. Only George Bailey could have understood the shame and helplessness felt by that executive at that moment, and I sure couldn't provide any angelic intervention to assist him in his time of need.

- *A **CUSIP** number identifies securities specifically U.S. and Canadian registered stocks, and U.S. government and municipal bonds and uniquely identifies the company or issuer and the type of security.*

It is true that, during the same period, banks were also offering similarly floating savings instruments. They, however, had a floating rate and much shorter term portfolio of investments. As their cost of funds rose, so did "their" prime rate and the corresponding yield on their loans. They also knew when to stop. They knew that when the cost of funds got too high that it was economically unfeasible to keep those deposits. They knew when it was better to let funds go out the door rather than to retain them at a prohibitive cost. They also knew how to make commercial and consumer loans and how to underwrite credit risk. After all, they were commercial bankers not rookie thrifts under fire doing their impromptu impersonation of bankers.

The commercial bankers had gotten just what they wanted. The thrift industry was on the ropes. A knockout punch wasn't even necessary. Only time was needed, and the thrifts were running out of it. The thrifts had done it to themselves, and the bankers were the strong alternative to the shaky building and loans down the street. It was now up to the regulators to straighten out the problem that the backwards deregulation of the financial industry had caused.

Chapter V
The Demise of the Thrift Industry

While all of this turmoil began to engulf the savings and loan industry, where were the regulators? Where was the Federal Home Loan Bank while its members were fastening huge boulders to themselves and about to go swimming? Where was the Federal Savings and Loan Insurance Corporation (FSLIC), whose job it was to ensure the safety and soundness of an industry along with its customers' deposits? Could the regulators have been caught as unprepared as the thrift industry itself was for this deregulation?

Well, early on as the signs of trouble began to appear, it didn't seem that the regulators had any idea of the magnitude of the problem that they had created. They did know that the FSLIC fund that would be used to cover any savings and loan losses was grossly underfunded if there were catastrophic insolvencies. Consequently, they tried a number of strategies in the early stages to minimize any drain on that fund.

One of their early attempts was the Management Consignment Program, or MCP. Since, at that point, the regulators did not have an army of people standing by that had the expertise to run financial institutions on a moment's notice, they tried to tap the personnel from other solvent shops to do their dirty work for them. And, as you might imagine, no one could say "No" to the very regulators that supervised their own institution. Consequently, the regulators would meet with the selected team from the solvent shop and train them in a "SWAT Team" approach to savings and loan management. Once a troubled thrift was identified and the decision to take it over was made, the regulators, along with the borrowed management team, would physically seize the administrative office of the target thrift along with all branch facilities simultaneously. Personnel were sent usually at the close of business on a Friday to all locations at the same time in order to avoid any last minute destruction of documents or other last minute improprieties.

The first thing that the regulators would do is to remove, legally and sometimes physically, all current executive management, usually senior management, plus the entire Board of Directors. They would then install their borrowed management team from the solvent thrift and they would vest them with all the necessary authorities to transact business on behalf of the regulators. This temporary management team would then remain onsite during usual business hours and would evaluate the remaining personnel. Usually all non-supervisory personnel were retained in addition to select management that had not been involved in the decision making process that had led to the thrift's demise. The regulators remained onsite for a short period of time after the takeover and then assumed an advisory role as support to the MCP team. During this period, the regulators searched for a purchaser of the acquired shop. This process, and final sale and transfer, could take as long as six months. I always wondered how, if this MCP team was so good, that they could afford to be away from their jobs for such a long period of time. Or, if the solvent thrift had so much excess management that they could afford to keep them on the payroll. Technically, this team still had responsibilities at their own shops, but the majority of their time was spent at their new temporary jobs. There were, however, some benefits to the solvent shop. They were reimbursed for the actual salaries of these designated employees plus a small percentage for their trouble, usually about a 10 percent bonus. In addition, and much more importantly, the MCP team had a firsthand look at the shop that they were managing. If it was a good deal, they would have the inside track on acquiring it. And, of course, it never hurts to assist the very regulatory agency that supervises your own shop. Unfortunately, later on in this saga, the regulators would use this leverage to their advantage at the expense of the same shops that had helped them.

The disposition strategy was quite simple. Don't use your own money, use other people's money. Unfortunately, investors were much smarter than the regulators. After all, they were businessmen who knew how to evaluate investments, not bureaucrats totally out of their league in the business world. In addition, since the regulators had been so difficult to deal with in the past, they had succeeded in driving away many qualified and reputable potential investors. Well, it became obvious that unless the regulators offered incredibly sweetheart deals, they could never lure these good investors back and the regulators weren't in a position to be that generous. So, if the good guys aren't available as target investors, who's next? The answer was anybody with money or anything that looked like money. All of a sudden investors were coming out of the woodwork. Builders, developers, real estate speculators, anyone that was tired of begging financial institutions for loans looked forward to having his own piggy bank.

At this point, I should digress and talk about just how a financial institution is bid and sold. This isn't like your normal purchase of any tangible commodity. This is a living breathing depository institution that has customers who continue to put money in their accounts and continue to make loan payments, every working day of the year. The shop had obviously been determined to be insolvent or at least woefully capital deficient. Simply put, if all its assets were sold, they would not generate enough cash to pay off all of the depositors. This may seem like a restatement of the obvious, but it is focal to what happens next.

The question now arises how do people bid for an institution? Well, there are two areas to consider. First, what are the deposits (liabilities) worth? And secondly, what assets will be used to fund those liabilities? Remember that deposits are an asset to the customer but they are a liability to the institution because they owe you the money that's in your account.

First, a bidder will decide just how badly he wants to buy the institution. He will look at the overall cost of its deposits, where its retail banking facilities are located, how these locations compliment his existing offices, etc. He will also look at the consolidation possibilities with his existing operations and the corresponding economies of scale. Secondly, he would look at what assets will be provided to fund these deposits that he will be acquiring. Then, after a careful analysis of both of these elements, assets and liabilities, he will decide how much of a premium, if any, he is willing to pay for those very deposits.

The higher the premium, the better the bid in the eyes of the regulators, since that premium will help to offset the amount of cash or assets that the regulators will need to use to consummate the sale. The next element of the bid is just what specifically the buyer wants in terms of assets to fund those deposits. The regulators would much rather give assets, especially since they are the assets of the shop being sold, rather than using cash that they didn't have to close the deal. In addition, since the regulators would have the job of selling those assets if they are not used for this purpose, it was always a much more attractive alternative to use them in the shop being bid. Bidders, of course, low balled the value of those assets so they got a good deal and a good deal more. The bids were then evaluated by the regulators and quite simply, the winning bid was the one that required the smallest contribution by the regulators. Obviously, there were other components of the actual bid relating to brick-and-mortar and other assets, but these were the main factors used in determining a successful bid. At this early stage of government disposition of financial institutions, neither the bidders nor the regulators were very sophisticated in this process. The investment bankers hadn't yet started to make their presence felt except in the largest of transactions. Their role in this deregulation comedy will come later.

Okay, that's the basics of the bidding process, but what does the investor have to bring to the table? If it's an existing financial institution, they already have quantifiable and verifiable net worth per their own financial statements which were on file with the regulators. And, if the acquisition doesn't dilute their net worth on a consolidated basis below required levels, they don't need anything else. However, if the investor is an individual, group, or a corporation specifically set up to buy the institution, sufficient cash or assets must be provided to bring the shop into compliance with net worth requirements.

Unfortunately, after most of the financial institutions had satisfied their acquisition goals, these private and sometimes non-traditional investors mentioned above had to be tapped. The regulators were closing more shops than they had good investors, or the shops, due to their branch locations, were unattractive to existing depository institutions. The Fed was desperate at this time and, as their own funds dwindled, they started taking investors who had anything that looked like cash. It could be almost any type of asset, whether real estate or something other. The next question was how to determine the value of these assets being put up as "equity" and the regulators had no idea. Shrewd investors were picking up savings and loans all over the country and using assets with very questionable valuations but that was all right (see David Paul and CenTrust in Chapter VIII).

The Fed had buyers for these numerous shops that they had closed, and that was the important thing. Or so they thought. For a brief minute I think that they really believed that they had performed the business equivalent of the "loaves and fishes" trick and they didn't think that they would have to revisit these same closure and disposition issues again, at least not on these shops.

The MCP approach was just one of the very early attempts that the regulators used to deal with this increasingly ugly situation. Another plan was the optimistically named "Phoenix" approach. This one employed the theory that if you combine a number of insolvent thrifts that it would produce something that might be more valuable. At the very least, you had just one large problem to deal with instead of a number of smaller ones. I don't think that even these rather naive regulators thought that anything of real value would rise from the ashes but at least it centralized a few things. One of the best examples of this approach was a small Chicago neighborhood savings and loan called Talman Federal. By 1982, as it was merged with Home Federal Savings to become Talman Home Federal Savings and Loan Association of Illinois, it had grown to be a $6,400,000,000 shop, a behemoth for that period, and had engulfed no fewer than sixteen area thrifts. Now at least the regulators had bought themselves some time. It would take many years to sort out the assets and liabilities of all of these underlying shops, and it didn't require the resolution of a single one until the dust settled. This method was tried in a few particular situations across the country but never really gained any great degree of popularity. The drawback was that it required a large number of financially troubled thrifts within the same geographic area to have it make any sense at all. And, although there were plenty of thrifts in trouble, most didn't meet these criteria. The regulators needed a better plan and so they looked into their magic bag and found the solution. Since most magic was really the product of illusion and mirrors, they would use the same principle. They would use mirrors, accounting mirrors.

Since it had become quite obvious that the number of well capitalized thrifts was not increasing, and those that were well capitalized wanted to stay that way, it was time to change the rules. What was needed was a mechanism to induce strong shops to take a chance on acquiring those that might just need a little TLC. You know the ones, sort of a "fixer upper." These were shops that needed merely some competent management and a little time and they would turn a healthy return to the acquirer. So, with just a little tweak of the accounting rules, the regulators invented the "purchase method of accounting." Now, if you took over a shop that had negative net worth, you could merely write off that negative spread over a long period of time. Up to this point, if you bought a shop that had more liabilities than assets, someone (the regulators) would be forced to make up the difference.

However, the regulators' well was running dry and they couldn't help facilitate anymore sales of thrifts if they had to ante up more cash. The healthy thrifts weren't about to say that they would take a loss upon acquisition of a sick shop. Usually any loss of that magnitude, which would have to be taken immediately, would put them out of business. So, using their new mirrors, the regulators now told these same potential acquirers that the negative difference really wasn't a problem. If you were a few million dollars upside down, just write it off over, let's say, forty years. Well, any financial institution that had any confidence at all in its ability to run a shop was sure that they could easily accept a small loss each year over the next forty. After all, they were getting a shop with assets and deposits. They could restructure it, grow it, merge their operations, and sell its assets and reinvest them at a much higher rate. This didn't sound like a bad idea at all, and it wasn't. Many solvent or marginally solvent shops took advantage of this new loophole. A large number of acquisitions were made, and everything was going fine. This loss that was carried forward was called "goodwill," an intangible and a prophetic misnomer. The dictionary defines "goodwill" as "the favor or advantage in the way of custom that a business has acquired beyond the mere value of what it sells." I guess that the regulators chose the proper word, but its definition was to change dramatically in the years to come.

Soon, however, some of the rather weak thrifts noticed that if you could acquire thrifts and use this accounting trickery, why couldn't you merely use the same approach on your own shop and instantly make it healthy? Wow, why didn't we think of this! If we just let you sell your old low-yielding assets and reinvest in higher earning assets, you'll be healthy too. Now we won't even need any of this thrift seizure stuff. We'll simply fix your shop, let you take this big loss and write it off over forty years. These shops contemplating using this method were basically good ones that happened to have a little "negative cash flow" problem and this could be easily fixed with a little portfolio restructuring and a little help from accounting. Taking this approach one step farther, in late 1981 the Federal Home Loan Bank allowed shaky shops to issue "income capital certificates" to the FSLIC. These certificates could then be included as capital and *voila!* the shop was now solvent.

A few months later, the regulators put the bow on their thrift present by changing the accounting standards that they used to measure net worth. The new set of rules would now be based on regulatory accounting principles (RAP) instead of the more stringent generally accepted accounting principles (GAAP). And, while they were at it, they even lowered the S&L's net worth requirement from 4% to 3%.

It looked like all of the thrift problems had finally been resolved and the catastrophe averted.

I watched as this evolution was taking place. After all, I hadn't been the one making these or any other rules but I was deeply involved with the various cottage industries that sprang up as a direct result of these regulatory changes. I had left my whole loan trading position and had become the Senior Negotiator for Fannie Mae in Chicago. I had thrifts in ten states that were in need of portfolio restructuring.

During this period, almost every surviving savings and loan had either purchased shops using these new rules or they themselves had taken advantage of the new options allowed to them. As a result, it seemed that every shop had old low-yielding loans to sell and would shortly have a pocket full of cash to spend on newer higher yielding investments.

I don't think that it is unnecessary to restate that the surviving thrifts of this time were still being run by executives that had primarily been raised in a totally regulated environment. Yes, their shops had survived the first cut, but they still had been involved in this new deregulation for only a handful of years. They had learned some things, but they could not have taken enough classes to give them the tools that they needed to deal with this constantly changing regulatory era. I don't think that many of that generation of executives could have, then or even now, made the transition necessary to cope. What was required was a complete abandonment of all of the principles that they had been taught. It required the replacement of all of their devoted minions with people that were familiar with this new game. It was necessary at that time to hire accountants that understood the game, investment bankers that knew the "street," and yes, even commercial bankers that understood lending. Unfortunately, the investment bankers were making too much money, the commercial bankers were having too much fun watching the thrifts flounder and picking up their broken pieces, and the accountants were still reading their new books. It was tough to find good help then even if you were that rare visionary that realized that it was needed.

Now, as well as then, there is nothing that investment bankers like more that an unsophisticated customer with a lot of money. These regulatory changes had created huge pools of assets being controlled by an aging and ill-equipped group that was not only motivated to sell but also motivated to buy. After all, they knew that they had to do the complete restructure game in order to book that loss that they would then start to amortize over that forty-year period. Wall Street knew that they had a rare opportunity to make tons of money on both sides, and there was no way that they were going to pass up their chance. The thrifts knew that they didn't even have the expertise to analyze what they had to sell so they looked to the "Street" for help. The large shops were the first ones to be put in Wall Street's crosshairs. A feeding frenzy ensued, one that I don't think will ever or could ever be replicated. Investment bankers of all shapes and sizes descended upon these thrifts with one plan after another on how to spin their straw into gold. Primary dealers, established regional dealers as well as some little known names appeared as if from nowhere. Each one grabbed a list of the assets to be sold and went to work. Usually they would each receive this information a week or more in front of a scheduled bid date. Then they would each crunch those numbers and come up with a sale and reinvestment scenario that they hoped would win the bid for their firm. Fortunately, for me and Fannie Mae, most of the mortgage product that they found was very seasoned and was prime fodder for an agency purchase. I would get calls from any number of investment bankers each requesting me to bid on the portfolio they had to offer. What they were attempting to do was to get a bid from me for any product that they found in my ten-state region and have that lender deliver it to me directly. This would take the investment banker off the hook on the purchase which he knew that I could easily consummate. He wouldn't have to act as principle and come up with cash either. He would just wait until I bought and funded the product and have the reinvestment instruments that he was selling ready for purchase by the thrifts.

At that time, we had rather exacting specifications for bidding a portfolio, and each investment banker was required to comply with our formats. However, the fun really started when we would have that same portfolio shown to us by 4, 5, or even 6 different sources. Since we required the broker to disclose where the product was coming from, we always knew when we had multiple bids on the table. It wasn't unusual for all the bids on the table to be mine.

Each one was based on how the broker sliced and diced the data and then how greedy he was on his fees. Sometimes it didn't even look like I was bidding the same portfolio after these brokers got finished with their number crunch. It wasn't unusual to bid over half a billion of different product per month and win almost all of what I bid. This same little drama was being played out across the country by other players, other shops, and other bidders. It was a bonanza for the investment bankers. Some of the more arrogant ones became so complacent about this buy/sell exercise that they hardly gave it a thought. One Wall Street minion (did I say Salomon Brothers?) even went so far as to leave a taxi running in front of the thrift while he transacted his business so he could quickly return to the airport and New York.

Maybe it was that my role didn't seem significant enough or maybe I just got tired of only seeing one side of the transaction, but I soon left for the investment banking community myself. Deep down I wanted to know what happened next. I had done the lending piece, the trading piece, and the agency piece. It was time to complete the journey and go from Main Street to Wall Street. The time was right, and tripling my salary had nothing to do with it…

During this period, things were looking pretty good for the regulators for a change. At least better than they had looked for quite a while. This little accounting policy change and the invention of "regulatory net worth" might have just fixed what was broken, even if they, the regulators, were the ones that broke it. If they had just left well enough alone... As you might expect, the accounting industry and their inexhaustible supply of Anal Retentive Bean Counters (ARBCs) couldn't tolerate any unauthorized tampering with their beloved Generally Accepted Accounting Principles (GAAP). I know that they put up more than a small objection to the regulator's new plans. After all, accountants were always right. They had literally written the book on this subject. They could never have been to blame for not disclosing that so many thrifts were insolvent. Someone else must have been auditing them, certainly not anyone from their pious fraternity.

Things were going too smooth. Rates had stabilized, most of the reinvestments that the thrifts had made were performing, and the regulators had a chance to catch their breath. Then four rather unrelated events surfaced that would mark the beginning of the last chapter in the building and loan drama.

First, those non-traditional investors that the regulators had welcomed into the thrift arena started to show their true colors. They hadn't made their money in the thrift business nor did they intend to. That wasn't why they bought the shop in the first place. The thrift was merely a convenient vehicle to use to meet their primary business objectives. These objectives ran the whole gamut of speculative investments. Though mostly real estate-related, no prudent lender would have ever lent money on the projects that they now found so easy to fund with their own money source. Unfortunately, there was a reason that other prudent lenders would not have lent money on these investments, and devastating defaults that followed showed this to be true. There was no check and balance system in place when the owner of the thrift made all of the decisions and his self-serving interests always came first. Loans for acquisition and development on questionable projects, land loans with inflated values, and blatant misuse of funds became common place. These thrift entrepreneurs had become bulletproof, or so they thought. In one case, a successful builder and developer who had purchased a thrift thought nothing of buying $50 million in third-party auto paper from Florida. He soon discovered that he was lucky to even have vehicles behind the paper let alone collateral of sufficient value. Since he had insurance against fraud and misrepresentation, he didn't even bother to perform adequate due diligence on the loans that he was buying. Well, as you might imagine, after the first $500,000 of fraud claims paid, the insurance company bailed out. What was left was a junkyard in central Florida with rusted hulks that represented the security for his loans. In his case it wasn't even fraud on his part that caused the demise of the shop. But that wasn't the case in many other thrift failures. Certainly there was fraud and a lot of it, but that shouldn't be the lasting impression on why the savings and loans are gone. There were many other reasons that contributed much more significantly to the problem.

Secondly, during this entire period, Texas and the adjacent oil states had been enjoying an unparalleled boom due to skyrocketing oil prices. And, as previously addressed, everyone wanted to share in their good fortune. Unfortunately, just as fast as the boom had begun, the collapse followed. Crude oil prices fell by nearly 50 percent, and everything that was built on oil riches began to crumble. The explosion in residential and commercial construction that had been the envy of all parts of the country stopped. The incredible growth that was fueled by oil and investment from almost every other state in the union now revealed an office vacancy rate well over 30 percent. This catalyst was directly responsible for not only the demise of the Texas savings and loan industry but a good portion of the problems nationwide. At the peak, losses at Texas thrifts accounted for more than half of all thrift losses nationwide and of the biggest individual problems, fourteen out of the top twenty were in their own backyard.

In response to this catastrophe, the Federal Home Loan Bank Board reached into their bag of tricks and dusted off the "phoenix plan" which had only been used on a limited basis, and renamed it the "Southwest Plan." The principle was basically the same. Take a group of shops, bundle them together, and sell them as a package to the highest bidder. This task, however, was enormous. By the time the dust had settled, 205 thrifts with assets in excess of $101 billion would be sold. But wait a minute. I thought that we already agreed that the FSLIC fund was about broke! Well, yes it was, and these shops couldn't have been sold if cash was required. Instead, the FSLIC tried using all kinds of cash substitutes. They issued notes, gave tax incentives, yield guarantees, just about anything except the real thing since their recent recapitalization wasn't close to meeting their ravenous needs.

The third event that was to help expedite the collapse of the industry came from the regulators. Since their patchwork of regulatory solutions seemed to be holding so far, it was time to begin to put the surviving thrifts on a firmer footing to prevent any back sliding of work that they had already done. They now felt that it was time to begin treating all shops just like banks, and they began to unravel the RAP bandages that they had place on the wounds of so many sick shops earlier. These bandages, which encouraged them to buy other insolvent shops and spread the losses for forty years, were now being phased out. They cut the "goodwill" amortization time line to thirty years, then twenty years, then ten years, and eventually they would be eliminated altogether. These new rules applied not only to those that had acquired shops in this fashion but also all of the shops that had done their own portfolio restructuring. Now they said, "Sure, that was what we told you then, but this is now," and just like that, they changed the rules.

The effect was dramatic. These shops were just beginning to recover after the first bout with deregulation and now they had the rules changed on them. This event would put enormous pressure on them to produce additional earnings and would set the stage for the final death knell of the savings and loan industry as we knew it.

The fourth and final event in this series came from the actions of yet another source outside of the industry's control. It wasn't from the new thrift entrepreneurs, the oil collapse, or even the regulators this time. It was from Wall Street. From the beginning the "Street" was there ready to give the industry a hand in using its newfound powers. Just as ancient kings bearing gifts, they would provide certificates from all over the country if you were looking for cash to fuel investments and growth. They showed the industry the marvel of brokered certificates of deposit and how easily they could raise money simply by picking up the phone. There was no need to put lengthy ads in the paper and methodically wait for customers to clutter up your lobby. All that was necessary was that you price your CDs right and they would deliver all the cash that you wanted.

This was the same group that was more than happy to help the industry spend its money when it did its portfolio restructuring and was happy to provide them with all types of "high-yielding" investments when it was looking for a positive spread. Now the Street was able to do both sides of your asset and liability management. They would bring you money and show you how to invest it and all you had to do was call.

But then the unimaginable happened. The rates that were required to attract all this brokered money got too high, and those "high-yielding" investments needed to make a positive spread got riskier and riskier. Soon those great-yielding investments started to tank.

Even sooner those investments that were called "high-yield" were renamed what they really were: "junk." Junk bonds, junk equities, junk was everywhere. This would be the final blow that would move Congress to create the new undertakers of the thrift industry, those who would perform the euphemistic savings and loan "bailout" or more appropriately "burial."

Chapter VI
The Birth of the RTC

This "bailout" of the savings and loan industry was nothing of the kind. This bailout was of the regulatory agencies that had supervised them. The costs had become astronomical, and no one, including the regulators, had any idea of just how much money would be needed to pay for this ongoing government folly. What was known for sure was that this was a very high profile problem and it was affecting every corner of our business and political life. This was an all too familiar scenario. Big business needed some regulatory changes that favored their business objectives, regulators were appointed by politicians, politicians needed money to finance their campaigns, politicians and big business formed a mutually beneficial alliance. Certainly this was nothing new. These types of alliances are prevalent in most areas of big business and certainly were not exclusive to the savings and loan industry. The big difference here was that savings and loans which were neighborhood fixtures were now disappearing and, at the same time, tens of thousands of people were being put out of work. When an event like this occurs in other industries it usually has local consequences and effects people in a concentrated geographic area as in the case of a plant closing. However, this catastrophe was occurring simultaneously in every state in the country, including U.S. territories. No individuals or regions were immune. The devastation crossed not only state boundaries but party lines, and everyone was being affected. In a few instances the individual states had tried to deal with the problems themselves. Oh, not because they wanted to but because they were forced to. This was the case in states that had their own state deposit insurance funds. States like Ohio and Maryland became early casualties in this battle, and their taxpayers felt the sting immediately. As in the case of Ohio, the hand off was made to the FSLIC but not until a bank holiday was declared and taxpayer money was put at risk. Similarly Maryland quickly exited this self-insurance game but not before costing its taxpayers $185 million. All other states that had been running parallel funds soon followed. Each had concluded that since they couldn't print their own money on the state level that this was a job for the only entity that could, the Federal government.

It was time that sweeping changes were made by the government. This cancer was creeping too close to home. Even high-profile Senators were now being affected. DeConcini, McCain, Cranston, Glenn, and Riegle, better known as the "Keating Five," would feel the political heat.

The New York Times

The Lincoln Savings and Loan Investigation:
Who Is Involved
Published: November 22, 1989

Figures in the House Banking Committee's investigation of Lincoln Savings and Loan Association of Irvine, Calif., and a related inquiry into five Senators who intervened on its behalf with Federal regulators. The Banker Charles H. Keating Jr., the Phoenix millionaire who as chairman of a home construction company, American Continental Corp., purchased Lincoln in February 1984 for $51 million and in-

creased its assets from $1.1 billion to $5.5 billion by 1988. Waged a five-year campaign against Federal regulators who opposed his direct investment of federally insured savings and loan deposits in real estate ventures. In 1986 and 1987, he gave $1.3 million in gifts and contributions to five senators. They later intervened on Lincoln's behalf with officials of the Federal Home Loan Bank Board. Lincoln was seized by the board last April; regulators have filed a $1.1 billion fraud and racketeering suit against him. The Regulators Edwin J. Gray, Chairman of the bank board from 1983 until July 1987, sought to limit direct investments by savings institutions and was sued several times by Mr. Keating. In May 1987, he deferred action on a recommendation by regulators at the Federal Home Loan Bank in San Francisco that Lincoln be taken over by the Government because of what they said were unsound lending practices. Mr. Gray told the House committee he was summoned to an April 2, 1987, meeting in the office of Senator Dennis DeConcini, which was arranged by Senator Donald W. Reigle Jr. Mr. Gray said Mr. DeConcini asked him "on behalf of their friend and contributor" at Lincoln to rescind a regulation curbing direct investments by savings institutions. Mr. Gray arranged a two-hour meeting a week later in Mr. DeConcini's office between five Senators and San Francisco Home Loan Bank officials trying to close Lincoln.

 M. Danny Wall succeeded Mr. Gray as Chairman of the bank board. He has been the chief target of the House Banking Committee's chairman, Representative Henry B. Gonzolez, who last month asked President Bush to dismiss him. Mr. Wall has said the board did not follow the San Francisco offi-

cials' recommendation to seize Lincoln because proof was insufficient to justify the action. The Senator Dennis DeConcini , democrat from Arizona, in April 1987, held two meeting between savings institutions regulators and other Senators in his office. Mr. DeConcini received $48,100 from Mr. Keating and his associates for 1988 re-election campaign but announced two months ago he would return the money. Early this year he called Mr. Wall and California state regulators urging approval for Mr. Keating to sell Lincoln as an alternative to the Government's seizing it. Mr. DeConcini has denied Mr. Gray's account of the April 2 meeting. Alan Cranston, democrat from California, met with Mr. Gray on April 2, 1987, and the following week with San Francisco examiners, both in Mr. DeConcini's office. Mr. Cranston also called Mr. Wall and California regulators earlier this year urging approval for Mr. Keating to sell Lincoln. For his 1986 re-election campaign, Mr. Cranston received $39,000 from Mr. Keating and his associates. Mr. Keating donated $850,000 to groups Mr. Cranston controlled or founded and $85,000 for the California Democratic Party. John McCain, republican of Arizona, attended the April 2 and April 9 meetings in Mr. DeConcini's office. He received $112,000 in campaign contributions from Mr. Keating and his associates. Mr. McCain said earlier this year he was reimbursing American Continental $13,433 for flights he and his family took aboard Mr. Keating's planes to and from the Bahamas in 1984-86. John Glenn, democrat from Ohio, also attended the April 2 and April 9 meetings in Mr. DeConcini's office, where regulators quoted him as telling them to either make a case against Lincoln or "get off its back." A candidate for his party's Pres-

idential nomination in 1984, he received $34,000 in direct political contributions from Mr. Keating and his associates and a political action committee associated with Mr. Glenn received another $200,000. Donald W. Riegle Jr., democrat from Michigan, met several times in 1987 with Mr. Keating or his associates and, according to Mr. Gray, first told him that he would be summoned to the April 2 meeting in Mr. DeConcini's office. Mr. Riegle did not attend that meeting. He was present at a meeting on April 9 with San Francisco regulators. Mr. Riegle received $76,100 from Mr. Keating and his associates for his 1988 re-election campaign but announced later he was returning the money.

• • •

And, as we would find out much later, those embers would continue to smolder well into 1996 and come much too close to even a President of the United States.

The New York Times

THE 1992 CAMPAIGN: Personal Finances; Clintons Joined S&L Operator in an Ozark Real-Estate Venture
By JEFF GERTH,
Published: March 8, 1992

WASHINGTON, March 7— *Bill Clinton and his wife were business partners with the owner of a failing savings and loan association that was subject to state regulation early in his tenure as Governor of Arkansas, records show.*

The partnership, a real estate joint venture that was de-

veloping land in the Ozarks, involved the Clintons and James B. McDougal, a former Clinton aide turned developer. It started in 1978, and at times money from Mr. McDougal's savings and loan was used to subsidize it. The corporation continues to this day, but does not appear to be active.

Mr. McDougal gave a detailed account of his relationship in several interviews in the last two weeks. This account, along with an examination of related local, state and Federal records and interviews with dozens of others in Arkansas, found the following:

*Available records covering the most active period of the real estate corporation, called Whitewater Development, appear to show that Mr. McDougal heavily subsidized it, insuring that the Clintons were under little financial risk in what turned out to be an unsuccessful enterprise. The corporation bought 200 acres of Ozark Mountain vacation property and planned to sell it in lots. During this period, the Clintons appear to have invested little money, so stood to lose little if the venture failed, but might have cashed in on their fifty percent interest if it had done well.

*The Clintons and Mr. McDougal disagree about what happened to Whitewater's records. Mr. McDougal says that at Mr. Clinton's request they were delivered to the Governor's mansion. The Clintons say many of them have disappeared. Many questions about the enterprise cannot be fully answered without the records.

*After Federal regulators found that Mr. McDougal's savings institution, Madison Guaranty, was insolvent, meaning it faced possible closure by the state, Mr. Clinton appointed a new state securities commissioner, who had been *a lawyer in a firm that represented the savings and loan. Mr. Clinton and the commissioner deny giving any preferential treatment. The new commissioner approved two novel proposals to help the savings and loan that were offered by Hillary Clinton, Governor Clinton's wife and a lawyer. She and her firm had been retained to represent the association.*

*The Clintons improperly deducted at least $5,000 on their personal tax returns in 1984 and 1985 for interest paid on a portion of at least $30,000 in bank loan payments that Whitewater made for them. The deductions saved them about $1,000 in taxes, but since the error was more than three years ago, Internal Revenue Service regulations do not require the Clintons to pay.

The complicated relationship between Mr. McDougal and the Clintons came to light in an investigation by The New York Times of the Clintons' tax records and business relationships. It raises questions of whether a governor should be involved in a business deal with the owner of a business regulated by the state and whether, having done so, the governor's wife through her law firm should be receiving legal fees for work done for the business.

Confusion Is Cited

Asked about these matters, the Clintons retained two lawyers to answer questions. The lawyers said the improper tax deductions were honest errors, made because there was confusion over who really owned a certain piece of Whitewater property and who was responsible for the loan taken out to buy it, Whitewater or the Clintons.

The deed for the land and the loan papers are all in the Clintons' names.

The lawyers said they were not in a position to answer questions about where the money that went into Whitewater came from. But generally, they said they thought neither the Clintons nor Mr. McDougal had profited from the venture. They also said the Clintons were once liable for about $100,000 in bank loans that financed Whitewater's original purchase of land. But the lawyers have only been able to find original documents showing $5,000 that the Clintons paid.

Some questions about the relationship and the Clintons' role in it may be difficult to resolve because of differing accounts and the missing records.

The two lawyers representing the Clintons are Susan P. Thomases, a longtime friend, and Loretta Lynch, a campaign aide, who participated in several hours of interviews at Ms. Thomases' Manhattan offices Thursday and Friday.

Payments on Debt

The records that are available, and Mrs. Thomases' account, show that Whitewater made payments between 1982 and 1985 on Mrs. Clinton's $30,000 real estate debt, reducing the debt by about $16,000 while also paying at least $14,000 in interest. At least one of those checks was signed by Mr. McDougal.

Mrs. Clinton originally borrowed the $30,000 from a bank also controlled by Mr. McDougal, Bank of Kingston, but "Hillary took the loan on behalf of the corporation," Ms. Thomases said. That, she explained, is why Whitewater made the payments.

The Clintons' 1984 and 1985 tax returns show that they took deductions for interest payments of $2,811 and $2,322 that Whitewater had made.

"It clearly is an error," Ms. Thomases said. She noted that the tax returns for those years were prepared by accountants in Arkansas.

The Clintons' gross income in 1984, as reported on their tax returns, was about $111,000 and they paid $22,280 in Federal taxes. In 1985, their reported income was about $102,000, and they paid $18,791 in Federal taxes.

Longtime Friendship

Mr. Clinton and Mr. McDougal had been friends since the 1960's. When Mr. Clinton became the nation's youngest Governor at 32 years old, he took Mr. McDougal into his administration as an aide for economic development. It was at about this time that the men formed Whitewater.

A few years later Mr. McDougal, having left government in 1979, bought control of a small savings and loan association, Madison Guaranty, and built it into one of the largest state-chartered associations in Arkansas.

But over time, the savings and loan got in trouble, like many others around the country. Finally Federal regulators took the savings and loan away from Mr. McDougal, and a Federal grand jury charged him with fraud, though he was acquitted. The Clintons were not involved in those proceedings.

Mr. McDougal began having personal problems, too. He was found to be suffering from manic-depressive illness, though he was judged competent to stand trial. In the interviews, Mr. McDougal appeared stable, careful and calm.

A year after the Clintons and McDougals bought the Ozark Mountain property and founded Whitewater Development in 1979, the corporation bought a modular house for about $22,000 and placed it on one of its lots. That lot was then conveyed to Mrs. Clinton, and the deed indicates that she paid nothing for it. Ms. Thomases says this was an error by Whitewater. The deed, she said, should have shown the price and said that Mrs. Clinton paid.

But the house was carried on the books as a Whitewater corporate asset and used as a model house to attract other buyers, according to Whitewater records produced by Ms. Thomases. Because the records are incomplete, it is unclear exactly what happened. But about the same time, Mrs. Clinton personally borrowed $30,000 from Mr. McDougal's bank to pay for the house and the lot.

Ms. Thomases said Mrs. Clinton and the corporation regarded this as a corporate debt, though it was in Mrs. Clinton's name. The corporation included no one but the Clintons and the McDougals. It was this debt that Whitewater made payments on until the end of 1985.

One year after acquiring the property, Mrs. Clinton sold it for $27,500, with payments to be made over time, records show. It is not clear who received the buyer's down payment of $3,000. But Ms. Thomases said it was the corporation that took the loss on its books. A few years later, the buyer went bankrupt and stopped making payments, and then he died.

In 1988 Mrs. Clinton bought back the house from the estate of the buyer. Records show that she paid $8,000 and then resold the property a short time later for about $23,000, *after closing costs. The Clintons reported a capital gain that year of $1,640.*

Ms. Thomases explained that the capital gain was small because, as part of that transaction, Mrs. Clinton had to pay off Whitewater's remaining $13,000 debt on the property, originally incurred by Mrs. Clinton. The payments the previous owner had been making to Whitewater before he went bankrupt had been used to help pay off that debt.

Account Overdrawn

It was during the period when Whitewater was making the Clintons' loan payments that Madison Guaranty was putting money into Whitewater.

For example, Whitewater's check ledger shows that Whitewater's account at Madison was overdrawn in 1984, when the corporation was making payments on the Clintons' loan. Money was deposited to make up the shortage from Madison Marketing, an affiliate of the savings and loan that derived its revenues from the institution, records also show.

It was also in 1984 that Madison started getting into trouble. Federal examiners studied its books that year, found that it was violating Arkansas regulations and determined that correcting the books to adjust improperly inflated profits would "result in an insolvent position," records of the 1984 examination show.

Arkansas regulators received the Federal report later that year, and under state law the securities commissioner was supposed to close any insolvent institution.

As the Governor is free to do at any time, Mr. Clinton appointed a new securities commissioner in January 1985.

He chose Beverly Bassett Schaffer, a lawyer in one of the firms that had been representing Madison.

Fund-Raising Ideas

Ms. Thomases, after talking to Mr. Clinton this week, said the Governor chose her because they were friends, and because he wanted to appoint a well qualified woman to an important post.

In interviews, Mrs. Schaffer, now a Fayetteville lawyer, said she did not remember the Federal examination of Madison but added that in her view, the findings were not "definitive proof of insolvency."

In 1985, Mrs. Clinton and her Little Rock law firm, the Rose firm, twice applied to the Securities Commission on behalf of Madison, asking that the savings and loan be allowed to try two novel plans to raise money.

Mrs. Schaffer wrote to Mrs. Clinton and another lawyer at the firm approving the ideas. "I never gave anybody special treatment," she said.

Madison was not able to raise additional capital. And by 1986 Federal regulators, who insured Madison's deposits, took control of the institution and ousted Mr. McDougal. Mrs. Schaffer supported the action.

• • •

Accordingly, in early 1989 President George H. W. Bush rolled out a plan that would provide a blueprint for wrapping up the savings and loan mess. A broad measure called The Financial Institutions Reform Recovery and Enforcement Act (FIRREA) was enacted and became the most important piece of legislation ever passed in the finance arena. This act immediately eliminated the Federal Home Loan Bank Board and the FSLIC in one stroke of the pen. In their place now stood the Office of Thrift Supervision (OTS) as the regulatory body and the Federal Deposit Insurance Fund (FDIC) as the insurer of deposits. We had come full circle, and now both commercial banks and savings and loans would have the same insurer of accounts. The last piece of this new law created an entity to deal with the disposition of the insolvent thrifts and was called the Resolution Trust Corporation (RTC). And, just to get the ball rolling, they were given a little seed money totaling $50 billion to get them started.

It became obvious from the start that the RTC had an enormous task in front of it but no one knew just how big that task would be or how much it was going to cost. What was also apparent from the beginning was that the FDIC could not possibly supply enough man power to perform this resolution function. But where could personnel be found that were knowledgeable in the ways of financial institutions and would be willing to work for a company that by charter would have a relatively short life expectancy? The answer was easy. Hire people that were just put out of work because you closed their savings and loan down! I always thought that there was a certain bit of irony in this practice, but the RTC needed people and these people were out of work and they would have to do. I'm not implying that these people had anything to do with the failure of the shops that they had worked for. On the contrary, they were not usually even the major decision makers in days gone by. But now they would be given an opportunity to manage some of the biggest individual thrift failures in the country and deal with some of the most complex financial issues ever addressed by the industry. Yes, they were quite overmatched by this task, but the FDIC wasn't any better. They didn't have any experience with the disposition of large numbers of financial institutions either. Nor had they been prepared for the diversity of investments and tangled webs created by the previous occupants of those executive suites.

What leads me to believe that the FDIC was unprepared for the task at hand was the rather quaint manual that they used as their disposition bible. As far as I could see, this was the only guidance that they had been given to them on how to perform their duties. It dealt with many topics that related to days gone by. It was a manual for a much simpler time. The entire treatment for the disposition of securities was one paragraph and certainly did not contemplate the types of esoteric instruments that they would find as the OTS referred shop after shop to them for disposition. Actually the only ones that were in a position to assist in the analysis and efficient disposition of the myriad of savings and loan investments were the ones that had created them. These, of course, were the investment bankers, and they were very willing to bid on any and all product but only on their terms. There was money to be made once again, and all they had to do was wait for these recycled thrift executives to call them and ask them to buy. Wall Street was ready to gorge themselves for a third time on this S&L buffet. The laughter was echoing once again between the tall buildings on that famous street in New York. The traders were poised to do it one more time, and they were the only game in town. Sure, the regulators wanted to hire consultants to assist them in developing a plan and telling them just what kind of financial animal they were dealing with, but when you're a consultant you can't bid on the product that you've been hired to analyze. There was no money in that. Let's just roll the dice.

Let's set the stage for a small S&L in, oh let's say Iowa, that has recently been declared insolvent by the OTS and the RTC has taken it over. Their first step would have been to appoint a managing agent (MA) to supervise the operation and disposition of its assets. The shop legally

Pottersville: Where Is the Bailey Building and Loan?

was put into Conservatorship with the RTC at that time. However, although they were not to begin mass liquidation of the shop's assets, they were allowed to sell assets to maintain sufficient liquidity and fund the day-to-day operations. Now let's say the MA sees some securities, bonds, equities, whatever and decides to sell them. Well, the "manual" tells him that he needs three bids to adequately expose the product to the market. Hmmm, let's see. I know a couple of guys from the Kiwanis Club that were always trying to get me to buy stock in one thing or another. They must know what they're doin'. I'll just give them a call. These little regional brokers or retail account execs for major dealers became the best source of product referrals in the early days of disposition. It was an easy way to buy product and bid whatever you thought that the market could bear. Once again, an inefficient market that will produce big spreads for the boys from Wall Street.

As I was to learn firsthand later in the story, the Street had its own impression of the RTC and put it quite eloquently as "They don't *R*esolve anything, no one *T*rusts them, and they're not really a *C*orporation."

Chapter VII
The Journey Takes a Detour

In early February 1990, I was on a consulting assignment for an established mortgage broker that needed some help making the leap to full service mortgage banking when I received a call from an old friend of mine. I had lost touch with him for a couple of years and I assumed that he was still making and trading mortgage product for a thrift joint venture group. To my surprise he had given up on the private sector and gone to work for the FDIC. Currently he was on assignment in southern Florida. As we got caught up on our respective activities for the past two years, he finally got around to the reason for the call. It seems that he'd been assigned to work with the RTC and they had just taken over a large thrift in southern Florida. Of course, in RTC speak they would never use such a crude term as "taken over." Rather the thrift was "intervened," making it sound almost like the government was doing management and the stockholders a favor to put them out of work and render their investments worthless, respectively. He went on to tell me that this thrift wasn't your ordinary savings and loan that took deposits, gave you a toaster, and financed your home for thirty years. No, this shop did things that were totally foreign to him and the FDIC, and nothing had ever been written in their regulatory disposition manual to cover what they found. They were doing things with names that only Wall Street could have understood, like collateralized debt, adjustable rate preferred stock, interest rate swaps, and junk bonds. This was CenTrust Savings Bank in Miami.

My curiosity had been more than a little aroused by the conversation and, not being one to pass up a free trip to Miami in February when the Chicago wind is howling, I told him I'd catch a flight out the next day. The next day was Valentine's Day. But I figured that my wife would forgive me just this one time if we celebrated it a day late. After all, I wouldn't be gone long. It wasn't as if I would be away from home for three years. It was only one night.

Well, what happened next I should have taken as the omen that it was. I had a limo pick me up at my home in a Chicago suburb at 2:00 P.M. for the twenty-some minute trip to O'Hare airport. The ride was uneventful and I arrived well in advance of my 4:30 flight. The weather was overcast with a little drizzle, not an unusual day for that time of year. However, knowing that in a few hours I would be in the 80-plus degree Florida climate, I didn't even bother to bring an overcoat, just a carry-on bag and my sunglasses. I was mildly surprised that within a few minutes, I learned that my plane would be delayed about an hour due to weather. Still not a problem, a small price to pay. However, as time passed, another delay and then another. Now, being a bit more concerned, I exited the airport bar to notice that wet snow is falling in a reminiscent pattern of Chicago snow storms past. This is not a good sign. As I struggled to wring any piece of meaningful information out of the artificial airline face in front of me, an announcement was made – my flight was canceled. As a matter of fact, all flights were canceled. What started as a minor drizzle had become what history would call "The Blizzard of '90."

Expressways were closed. No friends, family, or limo drivers can help me. I was trapped at O'Hare Airport with thousands of strangers from all parts of the world. They deserved to be stranded. They're travelers, they didn't belong here, but I lived here, only twenty minutes away.

I could tell that I was starting to panic, but wait, I'm a resourceful guy; in '78 I spent my birthday and more in L'Aeroporto de Leonardo DaVinci in Rome while the Italians went on a "one hour" strike. "Il strike" lasted a day and a half. But this is Chicago, not a foreign airport with armed soldiers guarding against terrorist activity, soldiers that I hope can understand my broken Italian. This is Chicago; I'll just get a room and wait for the storm to pass. Well, those "travelers," those people that "deserved to be stranded" knew how to travel better than I did; they had booked every room within walking or sloshing distance.

The thought of laying my head on the cold not-so-antiseptic floor of O'Hare Airport for an evening's rest, with my bed only minutes away, made me concoct a daring plan. With planes, cars, limos all grounded, what else can still be moving? Of course, trains. But there wasn't any train from where I was to where I wanted to go. Desperate, I took a train to the loop, downtown Chicago, that's where I'd find salvation. Not being very familiar with the train stops, I got off the train at the State of Illinois building and started to walk. The streets had turned from snow to that disgusting blend of slush and dirt that looked like an urban Slurpee without the cone. I knew that my walk was a good mile and a half, and with my wingtips weighing more with each step, I had to do something quick. Suddenly I spied a doorman at an historic loop hotel. He looked so dry and military in his red attire, that he gave me the courage to go on. I begged him to get me a taxi and gave him enough money to immediately spring into action. He flagged down a cab by throwing himself in front of it, the money had worked. The cab already had a passenger in it, but they saw that I was a desperate man. They let me in. As we plodded to the train station that offered service to the suburbs, I hoped that I would make the last train of the night.

It was almost a feeling of euphoria as I boarded the last train at 12:40 A.M. that night. I was going home and that's all I cared about. I hadn't thought of Miami or the sunshine in many hours, just my triangular odyssey around Chicago. I arrived home at 2:00 A.M. after a trying walk from the train station, I was cold and wet but I was home. My twelve-hour ordeal was over. I had taken a limousine, two trains, and a taxi, but not a one plane. That would have to wait for another day. So would Valentine's Day 1990. But I was sure that I would never miss that special day again. As I found out later, this was only the first in a long series of missed events covering the next three years.

Well, I ultimately did get to Miami but I don't think that I was quite prepared for what I saw and heard next. My FDIC friend picked me up at Miami International Airport and started to explain what he knew so far about this CenTrust Savings Bank as we began the drive down the notorious Route 95 to the central district. I say it's notorious not just for the number of disoriented foreign tourist that have been slain on this stretch of road but for Florida's own estimates that one-third of the residents don't have insurance in this "no fault" insurance state.

(By the way, if you have never been to a third world country, I suggest that you visit Miami International. I'm not quite sure what the predominate language spoken there is, but I know that it's not English. Every Central and South American country is well represented both by its citizenry and its sole airline. I have never seen so many airlines with names that sound like native dishes rather than a mode of transportation. The passengers though are quite seasoned. They were accustomed to doing their grocery shopping and using it as their carry-on luggage. I was sure that they could easily take an eye out with the protruding loaves of bread from their choice of baggage either paper or plastic. The only thing

Pottersville: Where Is the Bailey Building and Loan?

missing was a procession of goats and other livestock, which I fully expected to see any minute.)

Then, as if on cue, as we approached downtown Miami, I saw our destination an imposing structure ahead that dwarfed all the other buildings and dominated the Miami skyline, it was The CenTrust Tower. You know the one. It's the striking building that you see at the beginning of Miami Vice and most other shows filmed in Miami. At night it is illuminated with bright lights, many times colored, with a three-tiered effect as the smaller successive floors act as a color break to further add to its dramatic appearance. The lights surround it, all 360 degrees. Maybe the previous occupants couldn't run a thrift, but they sure could create a landmark building, and it was a fitting setting to hear the description of the task ahead.

I was whisked into a City of Miami parking garage which occupied the first eleven floors of the CenTrust edifice and into a fully caged executive parking area. This was obviously the secured area that was occupied by the former brass of the bank. A silent black stretch Mercedes limousine parked in the cage gathered dust as it stood testament to their security and largess. I would learn later that security wasn't a luxury but more of a necessity in this part of Florida. Off we went to the forty-second floor, near the top of the building but a lifetime away from the senior executive inner sanctum occupying the floors above.

I learned a lot about CenTrust that day. Oh, I had read about the takeover in the newspapers about ten days earlier but it seemed very far away then. Now I was hearing the facts, not just the debits and credits type but a story of incredible opulence, extravagant spending, perks, benies, deceit, and a blatant disregard for the rules of the game. This was the story of David Paul's empire. Paul was the Chairman, CEO and orchestrator of this high profile 8-plus billion dollar financial house-of-cards. During that period of FSLIC tolerance, Paul was able to take a

67

somewhat infamous commercial building in Chicago and use it to buy a non-descript savings and loan in Florida. The building was the 666 North Michigan building, the devil's building, whose address was finally changed officially many years later. Based on an inflated value of this less-than-landmark property, Paul was able to convince a very receptive FSLIC audience that he would take the troubled Dade County Savings and Loan off their hands. As previously noted, this was the era in which a mediocre baseball card collection could have accomplished the same feat. That little savings and loan was then grown into the largest thrift in Florida and the twenty-third largest in the nation. It became the legendary CenTrust Bank (notice the emphasis on "Trust" with a capital "T," another curious little irony in this banking saga). As it was later revealed, Paul, who became an icon in Miami society, bent the truth on a number of issues, not the least of which was his numerous academic accomplishments. Below are some excerpts of the David Paul saga and its conclusion.

Ex-S&L Chief Hit for $30 Million
October 22, 1990 | From Times Wire Services

The Office of Thrift Supervision said today that it will seek $30.8 million in restitution from David L. Paul, the former chairman of the failed CenTrust Bank of Miami. OTS officials told a news conference that it is the second-largest amount they are seeking in a savings-and-loan case. They said Paul's "insatiable vanity and greed" were a major factor in the failure of CenTrust, which will cost taxpayers an estimated $1.7 billion. The thrift agency said it is serving Paul with an order demanding restitution to CenTrust and barring him from selling or transferring any assets of more than $5,000.

Ex-CenTrust Chairman Says He Can't Repay S&L Funds
May 4, 1991 | From Associated Press

Former CenTrust Chairman David L. Paul, a national symbol of extravagance in the savings and loan crisis, says he's $3.5 million in debt, according to court documents released Friday. Paul, who has pleaded poverty for months, filed a personal financial statement with the Office of Thrift Supervision saying that his $4.9 million in assets are outweighed by $8.4 million in loans he must repay.

David Paul Indicted by Grand Jury : * Thrifts: The jailed ex-chairman of CenTrust Savings is accused of involvement in a sham purchase of $25 million in securities by BCCI.
February 29, 1992 | From Associated Press
A federal grand jury has indicted David L. Paul, the former CenTrust Savings Bank chairman, on fraud charges arising from the alleged sham purchase of $25 million in securities by BCCI, authorities said Friday. James McAdams, acting U.S. attorney for southern Florida, announced that a federal grand jury had issued the indictment against Paul, who was jailed earlier this week on contempt of court charges. The indictment listed counts of conspiracy and other crimes.

Ex-CenTrust Chairman Walks Out of Trial
August 4, 1992 | From Associated Press

Ousted CenTrust Savings Chairman David Paul walked out of his trial on federal civil charges Monday after lecturing the judge for 45 minutes about the proceedings, which he later called a "charade." The Office of Thrift Supervision, which is supervising the savings and loan bailout, is seeking $3 million in fines for Paul's allegedly improper money transfers and his failure to comply with its orders since his thrift's $1.7-billion failure in February, 1990.

Florida S&L Chief Convicted of Fraud : Thrifts: Former CenTrust Chairman David Paul used its funds to support his luxurious lifestyle.
November 25, 1993 | From Associated Press

Ousted CenTrust Bank Chairman David Paul was convicted Wednesday of federal fraud charges for using millions of dollars in thrift funds for his personal expenses while the savings and loan was failing. Paul, convicted on all but one of 69 counts, faces a maximum of 350 years in prison when he is sentenced Feb. 11. He was acquitted of one minor charge. Prosecutors asked that Paul, who is free on bond, be taken into custody immediately as a flight risk.

• • •

At that point, our discussion of the CenTrust legacy got down to some of the specific details of why the Fed was here and not the previous regime.

Sure, it was obvious that their liabilities exceeded their assets, I guess. But I always questioned who was doing the counting. I mean, all it takes is a regulator, who isn't particularly familiar with certain types of assets, to put an arbitrary value on them and put the shop on the takeover list. I'm not suggesting that CenTrust should not have been put on that list. It was by far one of the most outlandish examples of how "not" to run a regulated depository institution. I know that there were other instances where the regulators had no idea what they were looking at and, consequently, shops were ordered closed or taken over that were perfectly sound. In a few instances, where senior management decided to fight the take over as illegal, some courts reversed the regulatory action. **Franklin Savings** was certainly an example of this "fire, ready, aim" approach. In their case, management was actually reinstated for the better part of a morning while the Fed filed motions to overturn the reversal. Olympic Federal in Chicago was another example of a hasty decision. However, the court ruled that undoing what had been done would cause more harm than good to the entire regulatory intervention frenzy. Consequently, they let the takeover stand. Another victim of overmatched and undertrained regulators trying to make up for past mistakes. Not a big consolation to the ousted management that the battle was won but the war was definitely lost. (See the Franklin Savings and Loan saga below)

From Wikipedia

> **Benj. Franklin Savings and Loan** *was a thrift based in Portland, in the U.S. state of Oregon. Founded in 1925, the company was seized by the United States Government in 1990. In 1996 the United States Supreme Court found that this and similar seizures were based on an unconstitutional provision of the Financial Institutions Reform, Recovery, and*

Enforcement Act of 1989 (FIRREA). Shareholders of the thrift sued the federal government for damages caused by the seizure, with the shareholders winning several rounds in the courts. In 2013, $9.5 million was allocated for disbursement to shareholders.

Benj. Franklin S&L's television commercials featured its President, Bob Hazen. A short fellow with a high nasal voice, Hazen hawked toasters and other free gifts to woo new depositors and to pitch other financial products and services. Hazen is credited with inventing the thrift marketing phrase: "Pay Yourself First."

Hazen's father founded the Benj. Franklin in 1925. Although the name on signs and letterhead was "Benj." in promotions and discussions, the full word "Benjamin" was always pronounced.

Between 1982 and 1989 the thrift made a profit in 16 consecutive calendar quarters and became the number one mortgage lender in the Portland metropolitan area. It had strong lending positions in other major areas of the Northwest.

In 1982 the entire industry was on the verge of bankruptcy, as was the Federal Deposit Insurance Corporation and the Federal Savings and Loan Insurance Corporation (FSLIC), the government agencies that insured banks and thrifts to protect the depositors. Interest rates on savings deposits were over 15% at a time when the industry was invested in long-term mortgages charging about 8%.

When regulators seize a bank or a thrift, they find a healthy bank or thrift to "acquire" the assets, liabilities and customers of the failing enterprise. There are various incentives, including an accounting strategy that values the negative net worth of the failing thrift as a capital asset of "Goodwill" to the acquiring thrift. These were called "Supervisory Goodwill Agreements." The acquiring thrift was allowed to show this "Goodwill" as an asset for regulatory compliance purposes, depreciating (writing it down) over a long period of years. "Supervisory Goodwill" was also called "Blue Sky."

Absent "Blue Sky" most acquiring thrifts would be instantly out of compliance with regulatory capitalization requirements, so it was a necessary component of most forced mergers.

In 1982, Benj. Franklin was asked by the FSLIC to acquire a failing thrift, Equitable Savings and Loan. The agreement with the government included a 40-year amortization of over $340 million in "Supervisory Goodwill" ($644 million in 2008 dollars). Benj. Franklin and the government made a similar agreement in 1985 concerning the acquisition of Western Heritage Savings and Loan. These agreements had the full approval of the Federal Home Loan Bank Board.

In the middle of the S&L crisis of the late 1980s; the officers of several thrifts were accused and later convicted of defrauding investors and depositors. In 1989 Congress passed FIRREA. Critics suggest that FIRREA was a hasty reaction to the frauds and scandals that actually exacerbated the S&L problem, from crisis to a true disaster. Among its controversial provisions, FIRREA retroactively revoked agreements for the long-term amortization of goodwill.

The U.S. Constitution prohibits "Ex Post Facto" laws

(making something illegal after it has happened). In 1996, the U.S. Supreme Court found that this clause applied to the retroactive aspects of FIRREA.

In late 1989 regulators notified Benj. Franklin that the $330 million in "Supervisory Goodwill Agreement" phantom capital from the Equitable S&L merger must be removed from the balance sheets under the new FIRREA rules. Benj. Franklin was informed that unless it came up with a replacement for that $330 million in capital within about 90 days, it would be declared insolvent and seized.

The managers of Benj. Franklin pointed to the contract all had signed, and took the position that the new requirement to raise additional capital was a violation of that contract. They took the posture that they were in compliance and had a contract which defined compliance and did not need to come up with $330 million, roughly double the amount then held as capital.

Regulators declared Benj. Franklin insolvent and seized its assets on February 21, 1990 under protest. In September 1990, Bank of America acquired the thrift from the government In August 2013, it was announced shareholders would receive $9.5 million, or $1.23 per share, in a disbursement of the company's assets.

In 1990 shareholders sued the government for breach of contract. They've won in every contest so far.

In 1995, it was ruled that these shareholders had the right to bring suit "shareholder standing."

In 1996, the U.S. Supreme Court ruled in a companion case that the government had breached its contract for long-term amortization of goodwill.

Pottersville: Where Is the Bailey Building and Loan?

In 1997, a judge decided that the government breached its contract with Benj. granting "summary judgment on liability." Summary judgment means no trial was needed.

Trial on the issue of how much damages should be awarded started in January 1999, and finished in September 1999. Government experts testified that the damages to Benj. due to the seizure were zero. Experts testified that the value of Benj. Franklin at the time of the 1999 trial if it had not been seized would have been $944,000,000.

• • •

I spent the better part of that day in a corner office on the forty-second floor of the tower reviewing reports and documents describing a very lengthy list of capital markets assets. The office provided a breath taking view of both Biscayne Bay and downtown Miami. But what the documents provided was quite a different view. I had never seen such an array of bonds, debt, equities, mortgage product, swaps, and some things that I had no clue what they were. This wasn't your neighborhood savings and loan. This was a capital markets firm with a thrift charter. As I looked up from my reading for a brief break and almost as on cue, I noticed a sea of tombstones. You know, those plastic laminate plaques that Wall Street gives an issuer when they do a sizeable deal and generate a sizeable fee for the dealer. There were dozens around the room serving as a reminder that there were real stories behind these entries I was reading on the perforated green bar paper in front of me.

By the end of the day I was sure that I had had enough and wanted to give my FDIC friend the bad news. I was ready to give him my report, head back to the airport, leave the sunshine behind, and face the Chicago winter once again. As I began to describe what I had observed during my brief stay at CenTrust during our drive to the airport, I sensed that he really didn't want my report at all! What he wanted was me to work for him! I immediately told him that I wasn't interested. After all, I had a wife and three kids in Chicago. I could not possibly be expected to work in Miami and leave my family behind. And I know that they could not possibly move to Florida. After all, they had school and friends and a house.

My friend was unfazed by my logic. He was desperate and he was begging at this point. He was way over his head and had no one else to turn to. He offered money, a car, a luxury apartment, limo service to and from airports, weekly flights back to Chicago, and something called a per diem that I still don't understand. I knew that my wife would kill me but I agreed. Besides, it probably would only be for a few weeks, a couple of months at the most. I returned to Chicago to break the news to the family and pack my things. I'd be back to Miami on Monday morning to begin work.

CHAPTER VIII
CENTRUST SAVINGS BANK - Miami, Florida

Well, now you know what got me to Miami in February of 1990, but I should give you a quick chronology of events at CenTrust in its last year under David Paul. Events that got the FDIC to Miami two weeks before me.

1989
- APRIL 11: CenTrust stops the sale of capital notes at its branches.(Paul was selling this worthless paper as if it were an alternative to insured deposits but at a better rate of return)
- MAY 5: CenTrust ordered by regulators to stop expanding and to limit its junk-bond investments.
- JULY 18: CenTrust agrees to sell 63 of its 71 branches to Great Western Bank of California for $100 million.
- JULY 25: CenTrust Bank and its auditing firm, Deloitte Haskins & Sells, part ways.
- NOV. 9: Florida Comptroller Gerald Lewis releases a statement urging CenTrust to turn over its $28 million art collection to a third party for resale. Shortly after the announcement, however, CenTrust spokesman Robert Siegfried said most of

the collection had been sold that same day. He declined to say who bought the pieces or how much they fetched.
- DEC. 9: Federal Office of Thrift Supervision issues a temporary cease and desist order against CenTrust to keep its assets intact.
- DEC. 20: Regulators move to oust CenTrust Chairman David L. Paul.

1990
- JAN. 4, 1990: Carnival Cruise Line Chairman Ted Arison agrees to pay $100 million for eight CenTrust branches in Dade county for his own thrift, Ensign Bank. CenTrust stock price more than doubles, going from 75 cents a share to $1.87 a share.
- JAN. 17: CenTrust announces losses of $119.5 million for the latest fiscal year, with $97.3 million of the loss coming from charge-offs in the fourth quarter.
- JAN. 18: CenTrust merger with Ted Arison's Ensign Bank called off.
- JAN. 23: Trading in CenTrust stock is halted for a week. U.S. House Banking Committee subpoenas former junk-bond king Michael Milken to testify on dealings that involved CenTrust.
- JAN. 24: State deputy comptroller Larry Fuchs says takeover regulators have delayed taking control of CenTrust because of confusion on provisions of the savings and loan bailout bill.
- JAN. 28: CenTrust placed under control of regulators.

• • •

As I arrived on Monday morning at CenTrust Tower, I reported to the personnel office and was processed like any new employee starting any new job: lots of the usual forms to fill out with repetitive information for payroll, withholding, insurance, etc. Everything seemed strangely familiar yet I had never been through something like this ever before. I had just been hired as Executive Vice President of a savings bank, which on the surface would be rather routine, except this savings bank was dead. It was being kept on life support by the federal government until it could be sold, liquidated, or a little of both. I guess that it's normal when you start any new job that you think of your future and maybe your retirement but I quickly shook those thoughts, heck I would only be here a few months.

As I started to identify the other employees, the players, the government types, those that counted and those that were merely window dressing, I found out that of all these hundreds of souls assembled here, only one other person was brought in from the outside like I was. He was a good-looking guy, originally from Arkansas, who was about my age; his name was **Michael**. He seemed genuine enough without any obvious hidden agenda, just a guy here to do a job and get on with his life. But, I guess it's some sort of a Northern prejudice that many of us harbor, when you hear that slow Southern drawl, you just automatically put them in the Gomer genre, more humorous than effective. As I was soon to learn, that wasn't the case with Michael.

Evening recreation was rather limited. There were only so many beers you could drink, and even the local Hooters became routine when the girls know your name and look to you as friends. So one night we thought that a friendly game of "cut throat" racquetball sounded like a good idea. Shortly after, Michael, a fellow nicknamed "H.B. (who I will definitely cover later, if time allows), and I ventured to a local hotel to avail ourselves of their racquetball facilities. I was a fairly good 'B' division player having seen some tournament play, but I noticed that on all important shots, Michael could always be counted on to hit a volley-ending shot. Finally, after the match and length of time to catch my breath, I asked Michael if he'd played much. His slow response in his finest drawl was that he did happen to win the all-Arkansas title once a while back. This was my first insight into this Southerner's character and would prove to be the start of a long friendship.

A few days later, principals of one of the numerous commercial/business loans that had gone into default contacted Michael's group to arrange a meeting and possible workout of the defaulted credit. It wasn't a large loan but was in the five million dollar range. The meeting was to be held in New York and the principals, their attorneys, and accountants would all be present. We sent only Michael. The meeting lasted for the better part of the morning with the $300-an-hour New York attorneys taking the center stage. They painted a bleak picture of a company that would surely file for bankruptcy unless the debtor, CenTrust, agreed to a substantial compromise of about twenty cents on the dollar. Their case was intermittently punctuated with Madison Avenue charts explained and sworn to by the accountants and principals alike.

This was a well-choreographed presentation, and each part played to perfection. As they rested their case after about three hours, they looked to Michael and waited for his obvious concurrence, no other conclusion could be drawn except for the compromise they proposed. That group of Northerners assembled could not have predicted the chaos and confusion that followed when Michael took a deep breath and said, "Fellahs, that dog won't hunt." Hunting! Dogs! What the hell was this Gomer talking about? What kind of backwoods critter had the RTC sent to negotiate with this sophisticated group of businessmen? Well, I found out that day that Michael was not only a seasoned businessman and a veteran of many debt workouts, as well as a CPA. Now I knew why he was the only other "outsider" brought to this party, and I was glad that he was on our side.

In the capital markets area at CenTrust, also on the forty-second floor I found that I had inherited a group of young, eager, and well-educated credit analysts with impressive graduate degrees from University of Miami and Columbia mostly. They had been pretty well schooled in the art of debt and equity in the business world, and they were seeing its darker side while they followed about $1 billion of junk bonds in all stages of disrepair. As I interviewed each of them during my first week to find out just what I had to work with, that is, their experience and the specific credits that were assigned to them, I discovered that they were very sharp and knowledgeable for their young ages but that they had no real life experience. This was the first job for most of them. They hadn't had a chance to personally even own a share of common stock yet. And, as I was informed by the government folks on site, they were currently trying to hire more of these analyst types for my use.

Quickly, I stopped their search for more analysts and told them what I needed was a seasoned trader to bring some experience and reality to my little team of neophytes. If we were to analyze billions of dollars of complex assets, design a disposition strategy to optimize value, and then do battle with almost every primary dealer on the Street (all of whom knew my portfolio better than I did), I needed at least one capital markets veteran on my team to help even the odds.

Well, I did know such a person that could fill that role for me. His name was **Steve**, but I had two problems. I didn't know what he was doing and he lived in California! So, while I tracked down his current contact information, I was thinking about what I was going to ask him to do and how I was going to approach it. I thought that I'd start with making some small talk and we'd get caught up on what each of us had been doing and then I'd just blurt out, "How about commuting from San Diego to Miami to trade the pieces from a defunct S&L and get your butt kicked daily by most of Wall Street for a few months?"

I hung the phone up before I finished dialing. It struck me how insane that request would sound. I needed something better if I was going to prevent him from hanging up on me in mid-sentence. I guess that I really don't remember exactly what I said to **Steve** that day so maybe hearing it from his own unique perspective as a trader might be better.

By Steve the Trader:
Typically speaking, the difference between the best trade ever and the worst trade ever could be decided simply by the amount of money, goods or services gained or lost when the trade was done. But in this scenario, nothing could be further from the truth. You see, "best" and "worst" took on subjective meanings that went well beyond the pale of merely making or losing money. In fact, it was a foregone conclusion that we would lose money – the question was, how much? There are of course a myriad of reasons why this was the case, but the most fundamental of them can be summarized as (a) we could only trade the "sell" side of the market; (b) we couldn't do anything to either protect or augment returns from the portfolio; and, (c) the only time we ever were in a gain position was the result of some otherworldly market move that managed to erase all of the loses that might have resulted from a particular position.

So, one could argue that "best and worst" ceased to exist and instead gave way to a morphed condition simply known as bad. You may well wonder why the situation was bad (and often went from bad to horrific), or how or what events led to the creation of bad. Some of the reasons were systemic, while others were anecdotal. The systemic reasons largely centered on the fact that most of the people that remained with the shop were ill equipped to take on the sophisticated portfolios left behind by their predecessors, because the government supplied bodies didn't possess the requisite gray matter to fully comprehend the compositions of the inherited portfolios and thus lacking any real understanding of what they had, simply determined to get rid of the stuff as quickly, painlessly and quietly as possible; much akin to how someone might determine to have a mole or other irritant removed. In the absence of understanding, stupidity ruled supreme. The anecdotal reasons for why every trade was bad could be traced easily back to the methodology that RTC adopted for trading in the first place – but we'll get into that soon enough.

My Time at CenTrust Saving Bank
There are countless examples of abject stupidity run amok in this mass liquidation better known as the "Savings and Loan Crisis," but the following examples stand out as some of the finest.

I was young, but hardly impressionable when I got to CenTrust. I had been an institutional money manager, mortgage trader and had done some very early work on what ultimately came to be known as mortgage carry trades, and at the time of my hiring was managing my own money in San Diego. While I wasn't aware of it at the time, the circumstances surrounding my hiring I would prove perfectly suited to the three-ring circus I was about to join.

San Diego is what God made to reward the people he really loves – how I got there is still a bit of a mystery to me, but I digress. I don't actually recall the day, but the call came in from one of my very best friends sometime during the middle of March 1990 and I remember the conversation as if it happened yesterday. Skipping over the pleasantries, the conversation went something like this:

  Him: What are you doing?
  Me: Reading the racing form.

Him: (spitting out a mouthful of coffee) No, I didn't mean right this minute. What are you doing in general?

Me: Oh… reading the racing form.

He went on to tell me that he had recently accepted the position of "Head of Capital Markets" at one of the most stunning examples of hubris and failure ever created in the savings and loan industry. Though a mortgage banker by profession, he had been hired by a former colleague and tasked with managing the sale of several billion dollars of whole loans, mortgage securities, junk bonds and a plethora of other securities most people had never heard of. After culling through the surviving talent in the capital markets group only to discover that most of his analysts had never even so much as owned a share of common stock, my boss determined to set a plan to hire me. So, on the night UNLV beat Duke by thirty points for the national championship, I found myself on a plane from San Diego to Miami to discuss my job availability. Ultimately, I was hired because as he put it, he needed "an analytical trader with the hide of an alligator." Truth be told, he needed a lot more than that, but I was what he got.

"Seven days to trade $1mm in Treasury Bonds" was the first trade I recall having been made by our government handlers. I don't exactly recall whom they impressed into making that first trade (I believe it was someone that prior to his career at RTC he had been a retail stock broker with Merrill Lynch and thus should have known how), but judging from the aftermath of details, it was someone that had never traded a bond before. My recollections of the details (as told to me for I wasn't actually there when it happened) were that the person responsible for making the trade found five government bond broker dealers to bid the bonds. The dealers called in at the stated time and each in turn presented their bid. The bids were recorded, the calls ended and *that* was how the first trade ended. Securities didn't trade hands and the "trader" never acknowledged a winning bid. Each of the dealers were told that their bids were "subject" (a term used in trading that means we recognize your price but we are not holding you to that price, nor are you bound by that price until the seller declares the trade "done") and the phone call disconnected. I understand that the same person that was involved with the trade was told to execute the sale seven days later at what was the best price from the prior week. Seems reasonable, doesn't it?

For those of you who don't know this, treasury bond prices change constantly, and back in 1990 represented some of the fastest moving price changes in all the securities markets. To expect the prices to be held for seven days, much less seven minutes after they were presented underscored how totally out-gunned and out-manned that group in Miami were. That I became the new sheriff gave them only a slightly better chance going forward.

• • •

Before we get to the complicated capital market assets, let's talk about a mere piece of real estate and the difficulty trying to sell it. The following story sets the stage for what was to follow. Nothing was going to be easy. The landmark building that was to become our home for a number of months was built on air rights above a City of Miami parking garage, a concept quite foreign to the government types on site.

Miami's Showy CenTrust Tower Becoming a 47-story White Elephant

May 12, 1991 | By Leslie Wayne, New York Times News Service.

MIAMI — It is, without a doubt, the most striking building on the Miami skyline. Designed by world-famous architect I.M. Pei, the shimmering CenTrust Tower curves on one side, rises sharply on the other and glows in the nighttime sky. Real estate professionals call it a "trophy property," and millions of Americans know it from the opening credits of the television show "Miami Vice."

But for all its beauty, CenTrust Tower is proving to be a headache for the government, which inherited it in 1990 when CenTrust Savings Bank failed.

Three times it has tried to sell the 47-story building and three times it has failed. Now, CenTrust Tower is back on the block, for $50 million.

The government's inability to sell such a well-known property-the showiest in its $17 billion portfolio of real estate from failed savings and loans-is turning into an embarrassment.

And it shows how hard it is for the government to be a real estate agent: It is second-guessed by Congress, must follow cumbersome rules and has little flexibility when negotiating with potential buyers.

"CenTrust is a spectacular, landmark building," said Arnold Matteson, marketing director at the Barker-Patrinely Group, a Coral Gables, Fla., real estate firm. "But this is a very, very complex deal. And it is complicated further by the fact the government is very self-conscious about what it does and is being closely scrutinized on it."

First, the government tried to sell the building to the savings and loan that bought CenTrust's financial assets. But the buyer said no.

Then, the government decided to hold an auction, only to cancel it in a dispute with the auctioneer. Now it's looking for a broker to help. Within the last few weeks, the government has talked to several potential buyers and came close to selling it to one, but the two could not agree on price and terms.

Part of the problem stems from regulators' skittishness over making any decision that could later be criticized. But even the government's harshest critics admit that CenTrust Tower is not an easy sell. For all its positive attributes, the Tower has many problems.

To begin with, the government doesn't even own the land under CenTrust Tower. It belongs to the City of Miami, which operates a garage under the building.

That arrangement, rare for a major office building, discourages many buyers but was part of the urban development package when the building was erected in 1987 at an estimated cost of $160 million.

The building is also only half-occupied in a city awash in empty office space, and real estate experts say it could be years before it is filled.

Nearly 25 percent, or some 1.7 million square feet, of downtown Miami office space is vacant. Finally, the building is odd, a monument to the extravagant tastes of David L. Paul, CenTrust's fallen chairman, who drove the savings and loan from riches to ruins in a span of seven years.

"This is a complicated piece of real estate that the government inherited from a troubled savings and loan with a controversial chairman," said Jack Lowell, president of EWM Management and Leasing, a Miami real estate firm.

"And it's got some controversial holdovers from that chairman."

How many executive offices, for instance, have an executive bathroom with gold-plated sinks and a bulletproof shower door? Or an Italian marble staircase connecting four floors of offices with teak walls and mahogany floors?

The 7,000-square-foot executive suite for Paul and his top aides, in fact, looks more fitting for a James Bond movie than for corporate executives. The conference table is so big it cannot be removed without being dismantled. Electronic gadgets-televisions, tape decks and telephones pop up from the desks.

There's a working fireplace, gold-leaf ceilings and special air conditioning to keep the air a cool 68 degrees.

This suite is where Paul hung his Rubens paintings, dined on fine china and Baccarat crystal and oversaw a high-flying institution whose collapse may cost the government $3 billion. CenTrust was seized by regulators in February, 1990.

But such extravagance is not a selling point. The government estimates it could cost as much as $10 million to rip out such excesses and make these four floors more usable, as well as provide necessary tenant improvements to the other empty floors.

In the modest 1990s, after all, no self-respecting executive wants to be seen in such splendor. And a buyer would have a hard time leasing these floors to any of the hundreds of regional corporate offices set up in Miami. It would make their regional office a lot fancier than most headquarters.

One logical hometown buyer, the City of Miami, needs more office space but passed on the building, largely because such opulent quarters would not sit well with voters.

"The building is an inefficient use of space," said Kent Williams, a broker with Coldwell Banker in Miami.

• • •

Okay, maybe the building was a pretty inefficient use of space but it sure was striking, especially when it was lit up at night with three cascading contrasting colors. The Feds tried to shut the lights off and save about a million dollars a year in costs, but the city fathers and Chamber of Commerce protested. The building had become such an important symbol for Miami that shutting off the lights would signal that the city was closed as well. The lights stayed on and even changed with any appropriate holiday: Fourth of July, Gay Pride Day, baseball colors for spring training, etc.

Well, inside the building and on the forty-second floor, we were doing our own discovery of just what did we own. In Steve the Trader's own words, "We had a ton of junk bonds, mortgage notes and preferreds. Yen backed, reverse yen (reverse pearls), every kind of SWAP and SWAPtion known to man and layers of SWAPtions that ran nine layers thick." Okay I'll refrain from comment on the preceding since I really don't know what it means ☺

Anyway it was Steve the Trader's job to know what these things were. I needed to organize, manage, and keep this group focused on our main mission, and that was, to analyze, competitively bid, and sell a bunch of stuff.

(This was the group that was about to do battle with Wall Street. God help us!)

But I guess that my curiosity got the better of me as we worked through this portfolio. How did it get here? What was this capital markets firm doing so far from Wall Street disguised as a saving and loan in Southern Florida? I knew it wasn't David Paul. It had to be someone that had Wall Street credentials. My questions were soon to be answered when my Fed handler told me of a meeting with the head of the CenTrust capital markets division, Ron Dipasquale.

Well, that name surely rang a bell with me. This was one of Lewie Renieri's boys back in the Salomon Brothers glory days of mortgage bonds. Those were the guys that wrote the book on the topic and, whether right or wrong, made Lewie the father of mortgages just like Michael Milken will always be the father of junk bonds. I guess that I really owe it to Lewie for getting me to Wall Street via Chicago those many years ago. It was early 1984, and I was Senior Negotiator at Fannie Mae in Chicago at that time and was buying about $500 million per month of those whole loans for cash from S&Ls in my ten-state region. Yes, we were a little less than sophisticated back then with our little HP 12C calculators and some tables to do interpolation, but it worked. About that time Fannie in D.C. had an idea to do a mortgage backed bond. So, with the only piece of software that could do present value calculations, I put together a model for the bond.

Well, D.C. accepted my suggestions, and Fannie put the wheels in motion to take it to market. But, as soon as the news of our little bond offering hit the street, I could hear the howling and gnashing of teeth all the way in Chicago, and I knew that wailing sound was coming right from Lewie's office at Salomon.

Understandably, no Wall Street house wanted the 800-pound gorilla, Fannie Mae, in the market with a new product telling everyone how it should be priced and making it almost as efficient as the bid/ask on Fannie MBS (Mortgage Backed Securities).

The Street loves a market with little transparency, wide spreads, and where you have to call them for the bid/ask.

Fannie, being about as politically vulnerable as is possible, was immediately accused of violating its charter and probably jeopardizing the entire free world with this mortgage bond. We were in business to buy mortgages and plod along and not to be innovative. If we wanted to reduce the cost of homeownership, we'd have to find another way to do it, some way that didn't cut into Wall Street's profits.

It was clear that if I wanted to get deeper into the many uses of residential mortgages, it wasn't going to be at Fannie Mae. Then as if on cue, through a mutual friend I was contacted by Merrill Lynch Capital Markets. They wanted to talk.

It didn't take much for Merrill Lynch to see that I had a pretty impressive rolodex of S&Ls, banks and mortgage companies and a desire to create some structured mortgage deals. It didn't take me long to get blinded by a signing bonus and three times the salary I was currently making plus commission. I accepted.

I guess that at this point in my career I really didn't fully appreciate the atmosphere on a trading floor or the type of personality that it would take to succeed and prosper on one, but I was soon to find out.

How tough could it be? Merrill was only a block and a half from Fannie Mae on the fifty-fifth floor of the Sears Tower (I don't care how many times the building changes hands, it will always be the Sears Tower to me). I don't think that the openness of a trading floor had really struck me until on my first day at Merrill Lynch I first sat down at my assigned space and witnessed for myself the only tools that I was allowed to use, a shared Telerate screen and a phone. I felt naked, I had no privacy, everyone could hear everything that I said, I assumed even my thoughts were open for all to view. Where was the protection that I always took for granted that was provided by the walls of my office? All I had was half

Pottersville: Where Is the Bailey Building and Loan?

a Telerate (a Bloomberg to be added later) and a display of ninety-six push buttons on a phone bank linked to all areas of Merrill's mortgage trading floor in New York.

So I spent my days dialin' but not smilin' much and trying to hit some homeruns, that is, buying $250-plus million S&L portfolios to create mortgage bonds/CMOs * (collateral mortgage obligations), and while I waited for the right pitch (continuing with this tired baseball analogy), I'd hit some singles selling a few CMO pieces to my clients and even buying some MBS (mortgage backed securities) Fannies, Freddies, and Ginnies TBAs** from my mortgage banking customers.

However, I did get to visit Merrill Lynch New York for a few days every month and visit our mortgage group and our head of structured deals. He was a fella that I really enjoyed working with, and I believe he felt the same way about me. Since the general feeling I got from most New Yorkers was that no independent thought existed west of the Hudson River, I know that he treated me differently and even wanted me to follow him to Drexel when he later jumped ship, but I digress here on a number of levels.

On one of those many trips to Merrill New York, I met Ron Depasquale, who had recently come over from Salomon Brothers. I really didn't know anything about Ron at the time. Heck, Michael Lewis hadn't even written *Liar's Poker* yet and there were still many more chapters to be written in mortgage history at Salomon Brothers. Michael Lewis hadn't even referred to Ronnie as a "third string mortgage trader." yet. I personally never thought that. I thought he was quite a snappy dresser.

What I do remember is that Ron's contract was not renewed at Merrill and he was free to return to Salomon Brothers with his pockets stuffed with cash. I'm sure that Lewie and the guys had a good laugh over that one.

93

* CMO - A collateralized mortgage obligation is a type of mortgage backed security in which principal repayments are organized according to their maturities and into different classes based on risk. Income received from the mortgages is passed to investors based on a predetermined set of rules, and investors receive money based on the specific slice of mortgages invested in (called a tranche).

** TBAs – "To be announced" is a phrase used to describe forward mortgage-backed securities (MBS) and serves as a contract to purchase or sell an MBS on a specific date.

Now I can flash forward to my first few weeks at CenTrust in Miami. My Fed handler told me that Ron was going to be in for a meeting. It seems that he was still an employee of CenTrust Savings Bank, sort of. This seemed a bit odd since all other senior people had been physically led from the building on that Friday night last month when the Feds stormed the tower. But as it turns out, Ron didn't actually work for CenTrust but rather a shell subsidiary incorporated in Delaware. And since FIRREA, the Financial Institution Reform Recovery and Enforcement Act (the Act that gave the Feds their power) only extended to the depository entity, they really couldn't do anything to Ron. And since they couldn't really do anything to him, they asked if I wanted him to work for me. Okay, I did think about it for a brief minute. How I could put him in one of the glass offices and have all the screens and phones removed, and… No, a silly idea, and besides I still had all of his credit analysts working for me. So I respectfully declined the offer for Ron. But I did take them up on the meeting with Ron.

The meeting, of course, was at CenTrust Tower. I wondered to myself if Ron was going to feel a little awkward returning to the scene of the crime (I mean this only figuratively). But my questions were soon answered as Ron appeared at the meeting and began questioning each of us in the room individually as to our title and purpose in being there. I merely said "hi, good to see you" and that they had asked me to come down from Chicago to look as some assets. He let the Feds stay, threw the Fed attorney out of the room because he came without counsel, and the meeting proceeded. The meeting was brief and all was quickly resolved. Ron strategically took a token payment from the Fed, departed the CenTrust subsidiary, and closed that chapter of his career.

However, knowing that Ronnie had been there and he had been a part of this portfolio creation made me even more curious than ever to take a forensic look at the whys and wherefores of these investments and the master plan. But, alas, there was no time for that. We had work to do.

There were numerous trades over the next few months sometimes two or three times each week. Many of them probably warrant some comment like the 44 billion yen we had to buy one night at 9:00 P.M. ET in Miami to retire a yen denominated bond or other collateralized notes and bonds but I will pick only two trades. I'm sure that there were others that we might have gotten the better of Wall Street but they were rare. These two I know that we did win and that's what made them fun.

Next up on the trading docket was a $500 million notional interest rate swap position that CenTrust had entered into with Salomon Brothers. Obviously we had a substantial amount of triple "A" collateral behind this position that I wanted to free up. So, as we started the process of finding three counterparties acceptable to Solly (we had two already; Banker's Trust and Continental Bank had already made the cut – it's just fun to mention them), we get a call from Solly and they had liquidated our collateral and not at favorable terms as you might expect!

Yes, I know that it was obvious that we had violated the financial covenants of the swap agreement. After all, CenTrust was insolvent. Heck, that's why we were all here, but Solly knew what we were doing. We were just trying to unwind our position per the terms of the agreement and get our collateral back.

We were mad and wanted an explanation from Solly. So we asked them directly, "Why did you liquidate our collateral when you knew we were going to unwind the position with your approval of the counterparties?" Solly didn't hesitate and responded, "Because we can realize a $4 million profit and…we can!"

Well, enter **Jim the Lawyer**. CenTrust had an excellent staff counsel onsite, and we informed him of the recent events. Jim had us arrange a conference call with Salomon's traders and their counsel for the next day. As the call was about to begin Jim stood up and buttoned his suite coat. We reminded him that this was a conference call and they couldn't see him. Jim blurted back, "I've got to do some lawyer'n" and lawyer'n is what he did do that day.

Jim began by explaining in exquisite detail the recently passed act FIRREA (August 1989) The Financial Institution Reform Recovery and Enforcement Act. I especially enjoyed the part about the criminal penalties that could be levied against anyone found guilty of defrauding a federally insured depository institution. (I guess that periodically we had to be reminded that under all these exotic financial instruments was a savings and loan with some consumer's checking and savings accounts).

After Jim's eloquence, the Salomon group asked for a few minutes to huddle. It was obvious that the Solly counsel told the traders that we weren't fooling around and that we had a very big club. When Solly returned to the call, they asked Jim what we wanted them to do. Jim looked to me, and I said that I wanted to bid it out with three approved counterparties as I had said all along. Of course, one smart ass Solly trader blurted out the paste is out of the tube (meaning that the swap was unwound and the collateral sold), at which time Jim the Lawyer uttered the most profound words that any lawyer who ever lawyered has said, "Well, boys, you better get yourself a tube stuffer!" There was dead silence, and we knew that at that instant Solly's counsel was making gestures at the traders in no uncertain terms to do what I wanted. *

Well, I think Steve the Trader got Merrill Lynch to round out our mock bid and we knew that they didn't mind having some fun at Solly's expense. When the bidding was over that day and, of course, Solly had to be the winner (hell, we gave them last look), it would cost them $1 million more than they had planned.

> *The scuttlebutt that we got from reliable sources that day indicated that Solly's counsel, Brown & Wood, had informed John Gutfreund and John Meriwether (basically Salomon's number 1 and 2 guys) that they could easily wind up in prison if they didn't in effect put the collateral back. Ironically, both Gutfreund and Meriwether were both forced to resign the next year after Salomon's Treasury securities trading scandal.

The second trade that I would mention where I was sure that Wall Street didn't make us drop our pants involved over $500 million in mortgages at the Federal Home Loan Bank of Atlanta (FHLB). As with most financial institutions, borrowing from the FHLB was an easy and cost effective way to fill short term liquidity needs. But at that time, FHLBs required that physical collateral be delivered to them to back those advances to the financial institutions. As I reviewed the long list of collateral that they had provided to Atlanta, I noticed that it was all residential 1 to 4 unit ARMs (Adjustable Rate Mortgages) pegged to the constant maturity treasury index. Well, knowing that whole loans like these do not carry as much collateral weight because of their lack of liquidity and uniformity, it gave me an idea.

What if I turned these loans into mortgage backed securities that have a much higher collateral weight because they are totally liquid? So we put together a little agreement among the Federal Home Loan Bank of Atlanta (FHLB), the Resolution Trust Corporation (RTC), and the Federal Home Loan Mortgage Corporation (Freddie Mac). All it really said was if FHLB would allow us to take that $500+ million in loans and deliver it to Freddie Mac and then have Freddie Mac issue PCs (Participation Certificates), better known as mortgage backed securities and then have Freddie deliver those securities back to the FHLB.

So I sent two of my folks to Atlanta with ballpoint pens and a Power-of-Attorney to do some signing or rather endorsing of the mortgage notes. While they were doing that, I organized those loans in a very specific manner. I took all those with the lowest starting rates, margins (spread over the index), and lifetime caps (the maximum rates that the loans could be adjusted to) and pooled them together first. Then each subsequent pool or security included rate, margin, and caps in ascending order. What we had created was $500 million in high-demand securities in good, better, best order and the Street didn't know that we had them. They were brand new!

The least valuable securities traded first and we caught a good premium bid for them. Each bundle we offered increased in value and price until the last groups were trading north of 104. Yes, we knew this time we got very competitive and aggressive bids and had at least kept the Street honest on this one.

While we were doing our thing on the capital markets side, there were many different divisions within the CenTrust Tower dealing with a variety of diverse things from commercial loans, consumer loans, brick-and-mortar maintenance and disposition and, of course, facilities management. Somebody needed to make sure that the buildings are cleaned, someone takes out the trash, make sure the electric bill gets paid, etc.

Well, **Steve the Trader** checks in with a story he calls "Smedley and the Crawler" or the day our window to Wall Street got closed.

Pottersville: Where Is the Bailey Building and Loan?

But before we get to Steve's tale, I need to give some color on the protocol on the sale of capital markets assets and for that matter any assets where the FDIC had responsibility for supervising their disposition. Every asset that we analyzed and wanted to sell had to have the approval of the Credit Review Committee, a group of higher level FDIC folks that jointly had been given the authority to bless the sales. A rigid case format had to be completed including details of the asset and lots of other information. This case then had to be put on the meeting agenda in advance and presented by us at one of Committee's weekly get-togethers.

The meeting room was the ultra-luxurious one previously described on the forty-fifth floor where David Paul and his minions formerly met. It was equipped with every convenience you could want. Hidden panels that concealed rows of switches that controlled numerous hidden lights, motorized overhead screens, projectors, microphones, a huge mahogany table and posh seating for about twenty. I'm sure that David had his personal chef prepare some goodies for the attendees on numerous occasions as well. We, however, never even got a sweet roll on our numerous trips to the upper regions.

I learned early on that instead of presenting long laborious detail for each of these cases in the hopes of actually teaching these people what these complex capital assets were, it was much easier to intimidate them and have them quickly approve our cases so we would leave. Besides, they would much rather hear all about the $25,000 offer that they had gotten for that bank branch in Hallandale that someone wanted to buy and convert into a pet store.

So Steve the Trader and I would arrive at the designated time as our case was announced. Our materials having been previously distributed to the group so that they would have time to digest the proposals and prepare any questions that they might have.

Tom Pisapia

The first thing we would do is pry open one of those massive oak panels to reveal a huge white board as we talked about tracing the history of mortgage bonds to the creation of CMOs and REMICs and the impact of the Tax Reform Act of 1987. That was more than enough! Immediately I heard a cry behind me: "Move to approve!" "I second!" "All in favor say I!" "I!"

It was over that fast. I hadn't even found the markers yet and we were being asked to leave. So I slowly closed the hidden whiteboard without even making a mark on it, but it was a very powerful tool and, in the right hands, could be quite effective. I still believe that this was the most humane method of getting approval for both the Committee and for us.

Now that Steve had the go ahead to sell whatever the asset was that just got approved, it was up to him to contact usually five to seven primary broker-dealers and provide them all the information on what we were bringing to market. He would then schedule a date and time for the bid and confirm everything with the various traders. However, all of this prep work might take a few days or even a week to get set up. Now during this period our Fed handlers were very interested on market activity that would impact the value or more specifically the dollars recovered upon sale of that asset. That was the gauge by which all Feds on this circuit were judged.

And now back to Steve the Trader and the tale of "Smedley and the Crawler." **Smedley** was a well-meaning, somewhat hyperactive ex-banker, who by his own proclamation "Never made a bad loan!" which begs the question "Where is your Bank today?" but I digress. He was the individual responsible for facilities and accordingly was always looking for a way to reduce expenses, and a **Crawler** is one of those creatures that can be found in every office across the land; usually he is from IT or facilities management, and his job is to crawl under desks and connect or

Pottersville: Where Is the Bailey Building and Loan?

disconnect, phones, computers, printers, fax machines and sadly Telerates and Bloombergs.

Steve relates as I called in while on my way to a meeting with my Fed handlers:

> You   (standing in a phone booth in downtown Chicago): Where's the market today…?
>
> Me: New York!
>
> You: Stop fooling around, I'm standing in a phone booth on my way to a meeting and that will be the first thing they will ask me when I walk in.
>
> Me: I'm not fooling around…the Crawler was just in here and disconnected all of my Telerates and Bloombergs.
>
> You: [expletive deleted]

As I commented to my Fed handlers before our meeting began that I had no idea where the market was because our screens were gone, a very loud call was placed to Smedley in Miami and the yelling continued until the Crawler returned all of Steve's screens and the trading continued.

Over the next few weeks, as we continued trading and liquidating the remainder of the portfolio, we knew that we were nearing the end. We decided that we needed to have a party to commemorate this surreal experience. So as we prepared to set out for the local drinking establishment, we gathered up the dozens of laminate tombstones scattered around my office. Those tombstones the Street had given to CenTrust as a token of dollars raised and broker fees paid on each of those many structured deals.

But to me and my little group, those little tombstones each represented a deal that we analyzed, took apart and sold the pieces back to the Street, many of them back to the exact people that had created the deal. As was so appropriate to close this chapter, we auctioned off those tombstones to pay our bar bill. And as in keeping with the bail out that we were all a part of, it didn't cover the bill either.

At the end of June 1990 the announcement was finally made that *Great Western Bank* of Beverly Hills, California would be buying most of the CenTrust franchise; that is, seventy-one branch offices and over $5.2 billion of their deposits. This acquisition came as no surprise to anyone since Great Western had been negotiating with David Paul prior to his removal and had been willing to pay considerably more for sixty-three CenTrust branches in July of 1989. However, the regulators never got around to approving that deal so the taxpayers got the short end of this stick, as usual. This acquisition made Great Western the largest savings and loan in Florida.

CenTrust sold to California thrift
June 29, 1990 *UPI Archives*

MIAMI – CenTrust Bank was sold Friday to Great Western Bank of California, four months after federal regulators took over the insolvent thrift and ousted its chairman amid allegations he used the institution as his personal 'piggy bank.'

Great Western's bid for the Miami-based Cen-Trust bested offers from fifteen other institutions made to the Resolution Trust Corp., which took over the thrift in February from its lavish-spending chairman, David Paul.

Great Western, the second largest thrift in the nation, will assume all of CenTrust's deposits, totaling about $5.2 billion, the RTC said. Great Western bought CenTrust's 71 branches for $86 million.

'This sale of CenTrust reflects both a significant interest from Great Western and the aggressive sales efforts of the RTC resolutions staff,' said David C. Cooke, executive director of the RTC.

'We are very pleased with this sale and with Great Western's purchase later today of the Florida branches of Gibraltar Savings,' he said.

Great Western also obtained Friday 18 branches with $700 million in deposits from Gibraltar Savings Bank for $3.75 million. Gibraltar like Great Western is based in Beverly Hills, Calif.

The two deals will give Great Western 154 retail branch offices in Florida and deposits totaling $6 billion.

'Great Western is more than doubling its presence in Florida, one of the most attractive retail banking markets in the United States,' said James F. Montgomery, chairman and chief executive officer.

Cooke said the total cost to the RTC of the CenTrust transaction is estimated at $1.7 billion.

On Saturday, the RTC auctioned off paintings and other artworks, books, china, Baccarat crystal and Persian rugs purchased with CenTrust funds by Paul, recouping more than $300,000.

On December 20, state regulators moved to oust Paul, saying he 'maintained an opulent lifestyle largely at the expense of the association, and generally treated a federally insured institution and public company as if it were his own personal piggy bank.'

CenTrust, which was the largest thrift in the southeastern United States and the 23rd-largest in the nation, had total assets of $6.7 billion with liabilities of $7.5 billion, including $5.2 billion in 266,092 deposit accounts, the RTC said.

The failed thrift also had $2.3 billion in secured liabilities, including $500 million in advances from the RTC.

Federal regulators estimated that CenTrust's core deposit base is $1.78 billion.

The failed institution's assets include $783 million in cash and investment grade securities, $1.58 billion in one- to four-family mortgages and $928 million in consumer loans.

Great Western will purchase the $3.3 billion in CenTrust assets and will be given three months to review its purchase and return those assets that are found to have 'documentary deficiencies or that have specific defects,' the RTC said.

The RTC will provide about $1.8 billion to Great Western to facilitate the sale and will retain about $3.1 billion of the closed institution's assets.

Cooke said the RTC will recover a portion of its initial cash advances through the sale of assets to be held in the receivership.

Before CenTrust was taken over by federal regulators, Great Western had agreed to buy 63 of CenTrust's branches for $150 million. The federal takeover voided the deal.

Great Western first entered the Florida market in

1986, acquiring the failed Intercapital Savings Bank thrift of Jacksonville.

Two weeks ago, Great Western announced a deal to buy 13 Florida branches of Cartaret Savings Bank from AmBase Corp. for $26.5 million.

Paul gained control of CenTrust, formerly called Dade Savings and Loan, in November 1983, when it was $500 million in the red and near collapse.

He rebuilt the company's balance sheets and expanded the branch network while paying high rates of interest to attract deposits and using that money to buy higher paying, but often risky, junk bonds.

CenTrust fell on hard times in 1988 and 1989. Federal regulators told the House Banking Committee in March that the thrift's junk bond portfolio of about $1 billion appeared to have lost about $400 million in value, 'large losses' were expected in CenTrust's auto leasing business and there were $300 million in undeclared losses, known as regulatory goodwill, that Paul assumed when he took over Dade Savings.

• • •

So as the remnants of the CenTrust dynasty, including its remaining full time employees, transitioned to Great Western the new owner, I thought that I finally saw an end in sight for my personal odyssey. The thought that I could soon return to Chicago on a full-time basis and that I could resume some sort of a normal life was rather comforting. No more Sunday afternoon flights from O'Hare to Miami, sleeping in my own bed more than twice a week, and seeing my kids for more than a few minutes each trip sounded pretty good. I knew that I would have some work to do with the kids and the marriage to make up for all the missed time, but it would certainly be worth it.

But even before we could officially be laid off from CenTrust and, yes, get our severance pay (yes, severance pay ☺), I was asked through a friend to visit an S&L just a few miles up the road in Hollywood Florida to provide some assistance. This shop, Hollywood Federal S&L, had just brought in new president and they were working their way through some of the same issues that all the thrifts of that era were facing. They asked me to do an analysis of their mortgage operation in Hollywood, Florida, and of a mortgage banking subsidiary that they owned in Walnut Creek, California! I'm not sure that the current management had a clue as to why they owned a mortgage company in California, but they did and it had to be dealt with. That type of an outlier was always a red flag to the examiners for all the obvious reasons.

I know, I know – I was just mentally packing my bags to return to Sweet Home Chicago. But this little side trip couldn't take more than two weeks, max! So, I headed up route 95 in Florida for a week or so and then on to San Francisco and north for a few more weeks. In my travels I found a very competent management team at the Hollywood home office and a nice little mortgage company in California. I was about through with my analysis of the mortgage company and headed back to Chicago from San Francisco on a Friday. I figured that I could wrap this whole thing up with one more trip to the West coast the following week. However, on that Saturday while in Chicago, my beeper went off (yes, yes my beeper, this was the pre-cell phone era). I was a bit curious when I saw that the area code on the call back number was 305, Miami, Florida.

I knew that I hadn't left any of my belongings back in Florida; that was a closed chapter in my life and I had no reason to return, or so I thought. Finding a pay phone though, I quickly dialed the number. As the call was picked up, I had trouble hearing the voice on the other end of the phone. It sounded like a crowd of people were laughing and talking at the same time. Through the din I heard the voice of my old friend from the FDIC. It seems that he and his crew were busy the previous night. They had taken down the S&L in Hollywood, Florida, that I was currently working for. After their laughter subsided, laughter that was caused by my working at that mortgage company at that S&L at that time in California, I was told to skip the return trip to California for now and get back to Florida on Monday. It seems they were all concerned about that mortgage company so far away and just who was going to go out and handle it. They were all relieved to find out that I was already out there. They knew that I would know exactly what they would need and were happy to find out that I had already done a complete analysis and in their preferred format as well. And yes, they had to make someone the President of that little shop and I was the logical person.

As the weeks passed, I split my time between Florida and California, but always going back to Chicago on Fridays. But some comments about that little mortgage company in California. The FDIC folks just wanted me to close it down, fire the employees, and sell off the fixtures. I tried to convince them that we should continue to provide a warehouse line to them and sell it as an ongoing operation, but I was not successful. But rather than put all those good people out of work, I looked for and found a mortgage company in Southern California that was looking to expand to the North. And since my bosses just wanted the company to go away, I put out a "for sale" sign on all the office contents. Actually, of course, I hired a company to solicit bids for the furniture, fixtures, and equipment.

After the bids were all submitted, I gave that mortgage company in Southern California the "last look," that is, what was the highest bid. Not coincidentally, their bid beat the highest bid for the old furniture by one dollar so I sold them all the furniture and all the people that were sitting in the chairs as well. No one lost a job or a paycheck, and the Feds were just happy that it went away. I should have stopped my life right there, bought that little shop, and ended all the madness, but I guess I just wasn't smart enough to do that either.

Now I returned to Florida and found that there were still pieces of CenTrust floating around. One of the larger pieces was the CenTrust Mortgage Corp. a national mortgage banker based out of Deerfield Beach, Florida with a multi-billion dollar servicing portfolio. I had thought that the mortgage company had been sold, but as it sometimes happens, the deal fell through. Since this was a sizeable mortgage company doing over $150 million a month (pretty good volume in those days), the Feds had decided to extend warehouse lines to them by allowing three commercial banks to fund their loan production and to sell them as an ongoing business. So no, I didn't get to go home yet. After all, someone had to be the last Chairman of the Board of CenTrust Mortgage Corporation. And yes, I guess that would have to be me.

Well, after weeks of negotiation and lots of back and forth, the company was sold to Manufactures Hanover Trust, remember them? The old "Manny Hanny" that would become/get acquired by Chemical Bank and evolve into today's JP Morgan Chase.

Yes, this would be a fitting place to end this Fed odyssey on a high note with this sale of this mortgage company and get back to my life. But as I was packing my bags for the final return trip, I was called in to meet with the Regional Feds who not only worked out of the Atlanta office of the FDIC but also staffed a large office of the RTC (Resolution Trust Corporation), the FDIC's disposition and very disposable temporary arm. It was called the Southeast Consolidated Office or SECO in Tampa, Florida.

Chapter IX
Even More Savings and Loan Debris

After accumulating a number of business cards over the previous few years with seemingly impressive titles on the surface like: Executive Vice President, CenTrust Savings Bank; President, Plus Financial Mortgage; and Chairman of the Board, CenTrust Mortgage Corporation, I guess the Feds thought that I needed a real challenge, that was, join their club, take the oath, and become an employee of the RTC.

Among other divisions at the RTC SECO office was one called the Financial Instruments division. These some fifty-plus employees were in charge of the analysis and disposition of all of the financial products acquired due to the closure of, as it would finally tally, 104 savings and loans in Florida, Georgia, Alabama, Tennessee, and even two in Puerto Rico, along with all of their various subsidiaries across the country.

There were two Financial Instruments Coordinator positions at SECO, and one of them was vacant. I could see the handwriting on the wall. I really didn't have anything job-wise lined up in Chicago as yet and the savings and loans were still dropping like flies across the country every Friday at 5:00 P.M. So I met with the Director of the SECO office in Tampa, a savvy FDIC lifer who knew what was needed to get his ticket punched in the Fed system in order to move up to the next rung. He obviously did not have the mortgage or capital markets background to provide much detail but he explained the best that he could the challenge that was before me. Basically organize and supervise the twenty-five-plus employees in my group to analyze, recommend, and execute the sale of billions of dollars of diverse financial instruments. Instruments that he really couldn't describe to me nor the credentials of any of my soon to be team members. Oh yes, and I had about six months to get this all done.

It always struck me that when I had conversations of this type with government folks that no one ever mentioned optimizing value, finding the most aggressive bidders, beating the crap out of Wall Street, do the best that you can for the taxpayer, etc. No, just get this stuff sold and by this date and fill out the required paperwork.

I also knew that if I refused this appointment that I would not be offered another one. Yes, I could have returned to Chicago, unemployed but at least home. So, though reluctantly, I accepted my new title: Financial Instruments Coordinator, Southeast Consolidated Office, RTC, Tampa, Florida.

The real irony was that I had to take less money for this job, my housing expenses and airfares were on my dime now, and I couldn't get any direct flights to Chicago from Tampa. Fortunately, I had accumulated quite a number of frequent flier miles on American, but it would still mean that I wasn't going to see my family every weekend as before. Somehow it still seemed like the right thing to do at that time. It was a paycheck, and the market was still a mess.

On my first day at SECO, I was processed, photoed, and badged like any new recruit. As they handed me my RTC badge imprinted with a picture of me posing next to the American flag, I thought to myself how much fun I could have going in to any shaky S&L (and they all were shaky) and asking to cash a personal check with this ID. They'd probably give me their cash drawer just to leave the building.

Finally, I was allowed to meet my inherited staff. As I interviewed each of them I saw a very diverse group with varying skill sets as you would expect from a group that was picked up out of the rubble of all those crushed S&Ls. These weren't even the decision makers at those shops. Those people were suspect at the very least and deemed unsuitable for these types of positions. These SECO employees would be the second or third tier S&L players that surely had no role in the demise of their own savings and loan.

As I would later find out, this entire posting, interviewing, and hiring process would take up a disproportionate amount of my time. Of the twenty-five-plus people I met that day, only one guy stuck out. He was a savvy ex-mortgage banker and Viet Nam veteran from Cleveland. His name was **Tony**. I would come to not only rely heavily on him but he would become a close and trusted friend.

But in a repeat of that feeling that I had on my first day at CenTrust, I had no seasoned trading experience. No one that could help even the odds as we once again engaged Wall Street in a bidding battle.

In a scene reminiscent of Casablanca, "I rounded up the usual suspects." Get Steve the Trader back ASAP! Hopefully his roots did not have time to reattach to California and he was still in flux. Fortunately for me, he was available and he joined me in Tampa.

As I started to get my arms around my diverse portfolio and my employees' abilities during my first week onsite, my counter-part who was in charge of the other financial instruments group of twenty-five-plus employees, abruptly resigned! I don't think that I had anything to do with this action but I really don't know. But even our Fed handlers knew that there wasn't enough time to post for a replacement, process many hundreds of resumes according to the government protocol. That process would take months to even get down to a short list. They concluded that it would be better to roll both divisions under me. So now

I have fifty-plus people and more than double the assets to deal with and, of course with no additional pay or benies. Swell…

So, I evaluated the new members of my recently expanded group, merged them together and based on their individual skills, I put them into teams of four to six people to specialize on one or two specific and related instruments. I held mostly weekly, sometimes daily meetings with each of these groups individually to advise and monitor their progress. We had it all: mortgage companies, insurance companies, and a variety of other subsidiaries that either needed to be sold, liquidated, and/or just dissolved. And remember that earlier I mentioned that quaint method of selling off a percentage of a pool of loans and even keeping some of it for yourself? (See Chapter II, page 7) Those "participation" pieces numbered in the thousands and were in about every S&L portfolio that we encountered. Now, since those little fractional pieces were if not totally unsalable at the very least illiquid, we set out to buy the pieces that we did not own so we could reassemble those pieces and sell them as whole loans or pool them into Fannie or Freddie securities. And, as you might expect, Wall Street had figured out this strategy as well. Buy these little illiquid pieces on the cheap put them back together make a ton on the whole loan sale.

I had arrived back in Tampa from Chicago on my normal Sunday night flight on American and began getting ready for my work week as usual. On Tuesday we started hearing the standard rumors that the troops were on the move on Friday. What this meant was that volunteers would be needed to do an intervention this weekend. That always sounded much more civil. We weren't going to take over a savings and loan, put elderly executives out of work and usually forced into retirement, create penniless stockholders if it wasn't a mutual, make tellers and other minimum-wage employees cry. We were merely going to do an "intervention."

Just another unsuspecting savings and loan that would soon be put in to a panic. We knew the script all too well – but that wasn't the case for us! This meant overtime, paid travel and hotel, a $32.00 per diem, and, for some people, a place to bring a date. As the week progressed, it became clearer that the intervention was on. The name of the targeted shop was never divulged in advance for a number of good reasons. Not the least of which was the temptation to short their stock and go long their bonds. The RTC always paid collateralized bond holders and, if bought at a discount, could result in a hefty return. Not all the shops were mutuals. But enough of greed and the capital markets.

A number of my employees signed up for the weekend's activities for the above mentioned reasons. In total about 150 people were ready to move. This was about the right number. Make sure that we outnumber the enemy ten to one. Just in case a sexagenarian teller puts up a fight. This ritual organization was done with almost military precision. Every detail was checked and rechecked. It was a template that had been honed by being used many times before and since. The meeting time was set and assignments given out in manila envelopes. They were ready to go. This time it was a large, billion-dollar-plus shop in Daytona. Whoops, cancel the attack. We'll close no shop today. There's no room at the inn. Not one hotel or motel room was available in Daytona itself, nor for 100 miles in any direction. What could have gone wrong? All the Fed minds in Washington, Atlanta, and Tampa had concurred. But it's Easter break and college kids from all over the country have converged on Daytona, surfs up. The Fed can't be expected to know that kids do this every year and have since Annette and Frankie made movies. Those lucky thrift people don't know how close they came to losing their jobs. Oh well, what's another seven days, we'll just do it next week. Let's go bowling instead. And we did.

Tom Pisapia

I guess that the RTC didn't have the market cornered on mistakes made during interventions. I remember the story that a friend who worked for the now-defunct FSLIC told me about their experiences. It seems that they were also given marching orders to take a shop in a small town in Illinois. Since there was only one hotel, a Holiday Inn, the FSLIC booked a large number of rooms about ten days in advance of the scheduled Friday closing. By the way, all closings take place on Fridays usually at or shortly before 5:00 P.M. closing time. This gives the Feds the weekend to get everything in order for business as usual by Monday morning. Three-day holiday weekends are especially attractive for interventions. It gives them a little more time to prepare and, more importantly, and extra day's pay at overtime wages and an extra per diem. Anyway, when the manager of the local Holiday Inn saw his incredible occupancy rate for a dismally slow time of the year, he thought he should at least give some thanks. Accordingly, on the Monday prior to the arrival of his guests, he proclaimed his good fortune to the world. His marquee read in bold letters "WELCOME FSLIC," on both sides. Well, as you might imagine, word spread quickly in a small town. And, as luck would have it, there were two savings and loans in that town. And, since neither shop was particularly strong, they both had to wait all week to see which one would have company on the weekend. However, the FSLIC did learn from its mistakes. From that day on, they booked the rooms under the name of Arthur Anderson. Pretty sneaky.

On some of those weekends that I couldn't return to Chicago, I was also able to get involved with some of the RTC activities. I never did any of those S&L closings. I really could never bring myself to physically participate in closing an S&L. Besides, it was just as easy to have one of my people bring back lists of the financial instruments that I would need. But every once in a while, the RTC would hold real estate auctions. That was the other side of the house that actually dealt with brick and mortar assets. Residential, small commercial, vacant land, etc. and don't forget all those full-service branch offices of all those S&Ls that we picked up along the way.

If the auction was being held in a nice location, like Ft. Lauderdale, I might attend, approve the deals as they were sold, and pick up a few bucks as long as I was in town.

To put this particular phase of the journey in perspective, I knew from the beginning why I was brought down here. It wasn't just for my knowledge and work ethic; it was because I was expendable. These assignments were all "booby traps." If I did a good job and no one voiced any objections, I'd be given another assignment and another. If anything went wrong and, either a policy was violated or the public or the "Feds" objected, I was gone and became the scapegoat. I would become the cause and the only one responsible for the problem. It was easily correctable. I wasn't one of them, a Fed, just an outsider, they could never be held accountable for anything wrong that I did, only credited with my successes.

Now, however, I was one of them at least on a temporary basis and I had to make their goals for them. Well, there were three other RTC offices on the East coast and by the beginning of October 1991, our little office in Tampa had accounted for about 40 percent of all the sales, over $12 billion.

All of the appropriate FDIC people in Tampa, Atlanta and D.C. got kudos from their higher-ups on the food chain, got their respective tickets punched and now it was about time to close down this little financial instrument swap meet and move on. They had even praised *me* for all of my good work. I guess that it was safe now to say that since my last job was done. They even put me in for a cash bonus…$1,000!

But now it was time for me to go and I couldn't wait for those giant wheels of government to sanction my reward. I headed for Chicago and told them to keep the cash.

Chapter X
The Aftermath and the Future

I would characterize the rise and fall of the savings and loan industry as a sixty-five-year mortgage experiment from the very beginning in 1932 when the Federal Home Loan Bank authorized the formation of savings and loans to its phenomenal growth in the post WWII housing boom and even continuing to flourish until Financial Deregulation in 1982. The remainder of the history of the S&L industry is mired in finger pointing and excuses as we counted up the casualties and in 1995 found that the final tally showed that we had lost 1,645 (includes merged shops) of the 3,234 savings and loans or over 50 percent of our industry.

The surviving savings and loans that did weather the deregulatory storm didn't just disappear. I firmly believe that although they survived, they were exhausted from the fight and thought it was time to cash in their chips or maybe they figured that they dodged the bullet this time but the banks wouldn't miss next time. Regardless, there was one card left to play and most of them did play that card. Remembering that these shops were mutually owned, it was time to convert to stock ownership and do an IPO, initial public offering.

In Chicago, due to the draconian regulations on branch banking, there were literally hundreds of savings and loans and most of them who were large enough to justify the conversion fees chose this path. And, you guessed it, the broker dealers big and small were ready to take them public, for some hefty fees and a bit of the IPO stock for themselves.

An S&L's IPO stock was first offered to all of its depositors, which of course included all of its employees, management, and directors. Senior management and its Board usually had a big share of the deposits at these shops and they were positioned to get sizeable amounts of stock at the initial price. I did many a refinance for thrift executives needing cash from their home equity to buy as much stock as possible. This was the last sure thing, and it seemed that all of the IPOs came to market on the cheap and not only rose in value but many doubled and more.

I guess at this point I have to confess that I too benefitted in no small way during this wave. I diligently opened many savings accounts around Chicago at the savings and loans that were the most likely to convert, so that I could be on that IPO list. The bigger S&Ls that had converted were sitting on a pot full of cash and, as the smaller ones converted, they were easy pickin's for an acquisition. And yes, as stock holders it was a wonderful time too. Granted, the local banks could also pick up what they wanted or, if the consolidation produced a big enough prize, large regional or mega banks would take a look.

Not all thrifts went this way, but the majority did. Granted, some still failed, some converted charters, becoming banks or savings banks, and even a very few continued as mutuals, very few. The point is that even the term "savings and loan" merely conjured up some quaint concept from a bygone era, just a memory.

During its reign, the S&L industry directly employed hundreds of thousands of people in all fifty states and most U.S. territories, put millions of people into houses with long-term affordable fixed-rate mortgages, those homes became subdivisions and suburbs, city blocks and towns. Those houses created billions in value and generational wealth and a real estate tax base that grew economies on the state, county, and city levels. Those taxes were needed to build roads, streets, schools, and hospitals. Police and fire departments had to be built to support all those homes that the S&Ls financed and the people that lived in them.

If it weren't for the savings and loans, none of this economic prosperity would have occurred. The banks had no interest in putting thirty-year fixed-rate assets on their books and, for the longest time, there wasn't a very functional and liquid secondary market for conventional mortgages until Freddie Mac was created in 1970. Until then only Fannie was in the business of buying loans and primarily FHAs from mortgage bankers and large banks. But although the creation of Freddie Mac helped the savings and loans' liquidity and enabled them to increase the number of mortgage loans they could make geometrically, it did nothing to address the basic flaw of borrowing short and lending long. The S&Ls still had to meet the "thrift test" and have the overwhelming majority of their assets in residential loans and these were, of course, of the long-term fixed variety.

The little Regulation "Q" differential may have allowed the thrifts to attract more deposits than the banks but that certainly didn't solve the borrowing short and lending long conundrum. The only thing that kept the S&L business model viable was regulation. The deregulation of the financial industry was mass suicide for the thrift industry.

In the beginning of the book, I listed a number of possible causes of the "Savings and Loan Crisis." There were a number of contributors, but none of this genocide could have happened if it were not for the bankers, their lobbyists, and the politicians that were in the bankers' pockets.

If the S&Ls had just kept quiet and stayed in their place instead of trying to mimic banks, I think the banks would have let them continue to exist and play their mortgage game.

Sure, lax and underfunded regulators, accountants that were either poorly trained or paid off, crooked attorneys, and broker/dealers just acting like broker/dealers, all helped to accelerate the Banker's plan to wipe out the S&L industry. And they succeeded.

In the end I helped to liquidate some or all of the assets of 104 savings and loans of the total of 747 shops that the RTC closed. Adding the 296 S&Ls that were closed by the FSLIC, we lost 1,043 shops and an entire industry and culture.

The cost of this "clean-up" will never be known, but it surely took at least $200 billion out of the taxpayers' pockets and was unnecessary and totally avoidable.

Well, if you've had any trouble following this story so far, maybe I can help. It really covers some of the highlights of my forty-plus years in the mortgage business. I took mortgages literally from Main Street (Sycamore, Illinois) to Wall Street (Merrill Lynch Capital Markets, Institutional side, Chicago/New York) and back again. Along the way I made stops at Fannie Mae, The Federal Home Loan Bank, the FDIC/RTC, of course, numerous savings and loans, mortgage companies and, yes, even a few banks.

I took 3,000 residential mortgage applications with pen and paper and closed 2,000 of them at my desk with the same tools. I sold loans for cash, swapped for Fannie, Freddie, and Ginnie MBS, Dwarfs, Gnomes, and Midgets, did AOTs, CTOS and structured and sold pay through bonds, CMOs, and REMICs, anything that was anywhere close to a residential mortgage or even a convoluted derivative of one.

I think that I can bear witness to an industry that served the economy well and fostered home ownership when no one else wanted the job.

Well, not surprisingly, for the final chapter (fifteen years) of my own career, I migrated toward the credit union industry. Maybe subconsciously the credit unions gave me that same feeling that I felt many years before during my S&L journey. There was that same feeling of purpose and maybe a greater good. I enjoyed the references to the credit union "movement" and their mantra of great customer service and cooperation. The credit unions didn't even use the word "customers"; each was a "member," and they were part of something bigger and special. Plus, you had to "qualify" for membership. You had to come from the membership that the credit union served, perhaps a teacher, plumber, union, company, school, military branch, etc. Others were not even eligible for membership. Later, of course, credit unions defined their membership on geographic grounds as well.

But they all had to *join* the credit union and pay (deposit) $5.00 for that privilege. Credit unions even worked with other credit unions and formed Credit Union Service Organizations (CUSOs) with each other so that a number of credit unions could benefit by pooling their resources, for the common good of their respective members.

So off I went to Madison, Wisconsin, and CUNA Mutual Mortgage Corporation (CMMC), the mortgage arm of CUNA* Mutual Group, serving about 1,000 credit unions in all fifty states.

* CUNA (Credit Union National Association) – the oldest credit union advocacy group providing insurance and other financial services to help credit unions serve their members

This was one of the many mortgage iterations that CUNA had attempted over the years. They were always a company in search of an identity in the mortgage arena. I had called on them many years before because I could see their potential, but they were rudderless. Their current foray had involved bringing in new senior management, out with the old and in with the new, as simple as that. That left a number of vacancies so I filled a few of them – secondary, pricing, hedging and loan operations.

In the first year I did more trading than I had done in my prior life combined as I hedged a $1.2 billion mortgage pipeline and closed $4 billion in mortgages in 2003. But, as if on cue, in 2005, CUNA exited the mortgage business once again and sold the company. I spent the last ten years of my journey supporting the mortgage needs of credit unions (and a number of community banks) across the country with a company that I started at my kitchen table with the help of a number of my former employees from CMMC. What I learned is that I loved being part of the credit union culture.

There is a remarkable similarity between the savings and loans of old and credit unions of today. They were both mutual financial institutions; they work diligently to serve their customers, or members in the credit unions' case; they offer many of the same services that banks do, that is, savings and checking accounts, credit cards, auto loans, student loans, business loans and, yes, mortgages. But the credit unions serve their members like they are on a mission, and they are. The bought and paid for bankers cannot rival the credit union model and never will. Understandably, the credit unions are taking market share from the banks and the banks are furious with the credit unions and their tax exempt status and they aren't going to take it any more… The headlines blare:

Tax Battle: Banks on Offensive Against Credit Unions
Mark Koba | @MarkKobaCNBC
Wednesday, 11 Sep 2013 | 12:33 PM ETCNBC.com

Banks Pushing for Repeal of Credit Unions' Federal Tax Exemption
Bankers say the tax break is an unfair advantage for large credit unions. Now they see an opportunity to get rid of it as lawmakers begin work on a major overhaul of the tax code.
July 06, 2013 | By Jim Puzzanghera

American Bankers Association ®
Tax Credit Unions

Now is the Time to Eliminate the Credit Union Tax Exemption

Banks turn up the heat against credit unions

Bank Lobby Lashes Out at Credit Unions
By Silla Brush - 12/04/09 07:38 PM EST
Big Banks Push To End Credit Unions' Tax-Exempt Status

• • •

Wait a minute! Didn't I just write these same things about the saving and loans that were wiped out by the banks? What is to stop the banks from wiping out the credit unions in the same fashion?

Not so fast, Mr. Potter. The credit unions are not only better capitalized than the savings and loans, they are also better supervise by the NCUA (National Credit Union Administration *). In addition, the credit union managers are more competent and were raised under financial deregulation. And the most important asset that the credit union "movement" has is public support. I don't mean just the CUNA lobbying efforts and the support of numerous politicians, but the affinity credit unions themselves, the credit unions made up of the school teachers, the former and current military members, the labor unions, the state, county, and city employees, and the enthusiastic alumni at every university and in every state in the nation. There are just too many eyes in every corner of society to let those bankers get away with it again.

* National Credit Union Administration is the independent federal agency created by the United States Congress to regulate, charter, and supervise federal credit unions.

Well, I wrote the guts of this story in the winter of 1992-93 in a trailer in Wisconsin as soon as I finally returned from my FDIC/RTC odyssey, but I had to put it in a drawer until my finance career was over. It might have lessened my chances of getting hired in banking circles had it been published. But its writing was the catharsis that I needed to get my head straight and rejoin the real world of finance.

Now I am ready to pull the book from the drawer and fill in some of those gaps over the last twenty-five years and say the hell with banks! I don't need your damn jobs anymore.

APPENDIX I

THE TIMELINE

JUNE 1979 - Volker restricts the money supply and rates skyrocket from 9.06% to 15.2% by March 1980

Deregulation 1980 - Purchase method of account/ Goodwill/spreading the hit, no cash

APRIL 1981 - the prohibition on ARMs was lifted by the FHLBB for Federal thrifts

1982 - Garn-St. Germain Depository Institutions Act – allowed "Money Market Mutual Funds" (6 month MMC to rise with the market / eliminated the Reg Q differential / expanded investment powers / allowed brokered CDs

APRIL 1982 - elimination of the minimum # of stockholders and allowed the use of "in-kind" capital to buy S&Ls

JULY 1982 - extended the amortization of supervisory "Goodwill" from 10 to 40 years

AUGUST 1987 - Competitive Equality Banking Act (CEBA) – QTL (Qualified Thrift Lender) Test >>Needed only 60% of assets in residential lending to pass thrift test. Recapitalizes FSLIC with $10.8b

AUGUST 1989 - FIRREA – The Financial Institutions Reform Recovery and Enforcement Act abolishes The FHLBB and the FSLIC. Creates the RTC - Resolution Trust Corporation to liquidate assets of the insolvent S&Ls.

S&L crisis of the '80s and '90s – 1,043 S&Ls failed out of 3,234 – FSLIC dealt with 296 shops and the RTC with 747. I personally dealt with 104 of the RTC shops in the Southeast and Puerto Rico.

ESSAYS AND ARTICLES

Associated Press, "Ex-CenTrust Chairman Says He Can't Repay S&L Funds", May 4, 1991, p. 69

Associated Press, "David Paul Indicted by Grand Jury: Thrifts: The jailed ex-chairman of CenTrust Savings is accused of involvement in a sham purchase of $25 million in securities by BCCI", February 29, 1992, p. 69

Associated Press, "Ex-CenTrust Chairman Walks Out of Trial", August 4, 1992, p. 70

Associated Press, "Florida S&L Chief Convicted of Fraud: Thrifts: Former Centrust Chairman David Paul used its funds to support his luxurious lifestyle", November 25, 1993, p. 70

New York Times News Service, "Miami's Showy Centrust Tower Becoming A 47-story White Elephant", May 12, 1991 By Leslie Wayne, p. 85

Times Wire Services, "Ex-S&L Chief Hit for $30 Million", October 22, 1990, p. 68

The New York Times, "The Lincoln Savings and Loan Investigation: Who Is Involved", Published: November 22, 1989, p. 48

The New York Times, "THE 1992 CAMPAIGN: Personal Finances; Clintons Joined S. & L. Operator In an Ozark Real-Estate Venture", By Jeff Gerth, Published: March 8, 1992, p. 51

Turner Classic Movies @ TCM.com, Brief Synopsis of It's A Wonderful Life (1946), Prologue page xv

UPI Archives, "CenTrust sold to California thrift", June 29, 1990, p. 102

Wikipedia, "Benj. Franklin Savings and Loan was a thrift based in Portland, in the U.S. state of Oregon," p. 71